# Advanced Brilliant Writing

## Workbook

*Written by RITA-Award Winning, Bests-Selling Novelist*

# SUSAN MAY WARREN

**Advanced Brilliant Writing Workbook.**

Visit our Web site at www.mybooktherapy.com for information on more resources for writers.

To receive instruction on writing, or further help with writing projects via My Book Therapies boutique fiction editing services, contact info@mybooktherapy.com

# Advanced Brilliant Writing

## Workbook

**Susan May Warren**

Susan May Warren is the Christy, RITA and Carol award-winning author of over forty-five novels with Tyndale, Barbour, Steeple Hill and Summerside Press. A prolific novelist with over 1 million books sold, Susan has written contemporary and historical romances, romantic-suspense, thrillers, rom-com and Christmas novellas. She loves to help people launch their writing careers and is the founder of www.MyBookTherapy.com and www.LearnHowtoWriteaNovel.com, a writing website that helps authors get published and stay published. She's also the author of the popular writing method, *The Story Equation*. Find excerpts and reviews of her novels at www.susanmaywarren.com

# Dedication:

For your Glory, Lord…

To everyone who ever attended one of my classes, encouraged me and wanted more from their writing, this is for you.

# Acknowledgements

To the *My Book Therapy Voices* for their encouragement and questions that make me into a better writer and teacher.

To Steve Laube for walking me through the world of self-publishing! You rock.

To Beth Vogt, for knowing the Chicago Manual of Style and applying your amazing skills to this worktext. I shudder to think what it would have looked like without you!

To Rachel….*MY* Therapist.
You are brilliant.

Finally, to Andrew and my family.
You make me feel like a rock star.

Susan May Warren

# Table of Contents

# Introduction

I love novels. A great book reaches out and pulls me inside, subtly, makes me feel what the characters feel, and help me experience stories and events beyond myself. I can travel through time and space in books and experience what it is like to jump from a plane, or ride a bull, or fall in love, again and again. There is a magic in a well-written novel. Through it, I can revive lost loves, delight in childhood, become a Scottish warlord….and hopefully, in the journey, become a better person. I want to walk away pondering some truth.

But I don't want to be preached at, don't want the author to choke their story with their agenda. Don't want to be told what to think or feel. I want to come to my own conclusions and simply experience the journey with the character in a way that makes me examine my own journey through life.

How, as authors, do we help a reader connect with a character so smoothly that they become a part of the story? How do we make our readers laugh, cry and believe the story?

It's more than just words. And more than just structure. It's about creating a believable journey of change for your character, then folding that change into the story. It's about luring our readers into the story by revealing our characters layer by layer so that the reader longs to know them better. Finally, it's about wooing our readers with our sentences and words so that they stir the heart of the reader.

I read a lot of good books out there – books that structurally correct, that have a sound hero's journey and a sweet romance. But the truth is, as an author, I want more. I want to craft a story that captures a reader's heart, and changes their world in some way. In short, I don't want good….I want breathtaking.

My last book, **How to Write a Brilliant Novel**, I covered all the foundational elements of putting together a novel. I wanted to help people realize their dreams. But there is so much more that goes into a novel. If you want to make your book amazing, you have to think deeper with your characters, and wider with your plot. You need to go beyond the basics or the structurally correct and reach for more.

That's why, the moment I finished How to Write a Brilliant Novel, and looked at the list of topics I didn't cover, I knew I needed to write Advanced Brilliant Writing.

This book is designed to take your now-completed rough draft (or the outline for your rough draft) and make you take a deeper look at your characterization – from journey to implementation. You'll learn how to plot a profound character change journey, how to use backstory correctly and how to reveal your character slowly and for the most impact. Finally, we'll get specific and I'll teach you how to apply these changes to create powerful scenes. The questions and/or charts and exercises at the end of the chapters will equip you to build everything you are learning into your story.

The second section of the book will help you examine your plot. Remember those times when you throw a book against the wall? That's because a story doesn't make sense, or the characters are too stupid to live. I'll give you some techniques that will keep *your* books from ever ending up face down in a corner. I'll teach you how to drive your character through the story with the right balance of stakes and motivation, a way to widen your plot and make your hero more heroic with each plot step. You'll learn some tricks on making your plot more unique and compelling -- and the difference between Subplots and layers and how to use each effectively. Finally, you'll learn how to create the perfect Villain, and how doing so widens your plot even more.

As authors, let's not settle for good. Let's take our story deeper and wider…and breathtaking.

Susan May Warren

# Section One: Deep Characters

I believe a great story is driven by great characters. *Pride and Prejudice* wouldn't be a great story without the Elizabeth Bennett and Mr. Darcy. *Braveheart* would just be another war for freedom without William Wallace. Jack Bauer is *24*, and no one but Dr. Richard Kimble could have solved his wife's murder.

We love a character who takes a hold of us and becomes so real in our minds we can see them walking down the street. A character with whom we can cry, fall in love and charge into battle. We want to change with a character and learn their lessons.

For a while, we want to be them. Or at least be their friend.

But how do you draw characters that seem to breathe and bleed? And how do you connect them with your reader?

In my first writing book, How to Write a Brilliant Novel, I teach how to build a character from the inside out. To do so, you first ask the right questions based on the five areas of self-esteem. Then you build a plot around those answers. That method is the foundation for great characterization. But to really draw your reader into the life of your character, we as authors have to go deeper, have to engage our characters in an emotional journey of change. We have to layer our characters, so that when we reveal them we do it with the right balance and timing for the most impact. We have to write scenes that evoke emotions, with just the right amount of backstory. And, we need to connect our characters to our readers on a soul-deep level.

Going *deep* with a character is about going beyond the basics of characterization. Going deep is about pondering your character's journey and then thinking through how to engage the reader in the journey. It's advanced fiction writing, and if you do it right, you can build a story that won't just touch your reader…but change them.

Let's get started.

# Part One: Character Change Journey

## *Act 1: See the characters change?*

I love fall. I love the smell of decaying leaves, the sound of them crunching under my feet or as they trickle across the lawn, thrown by the wind. I love the colors – the blush reds, the pumpkin oranges, the golden yellows. The touch of frost in my nose in the morning. I can taste winter on the crisp breeze, and I know someday I'll awake to the fresh grace of snow blanketing my yard. Or, maybe it's just the change I love because, well, I love spring too.

There's something exhilarating about change, about the transition from old to new. It's probably what empowers us Minnesotans to endure the long months of winter (especially as it turns dreary right around March). And probably, it's that promise of something new that we offer our readers as they march through our books. (Hopefully without the use of the word "dreary!") They want to see how our hero goes from selfish to sacrificial, from a farm-boy to a warrior.

Every once in a while, up here in the northland, we'll have what was called during my childhood days of "Indian summer." It's when the temperature flares into the 80s for three or four days, after which comes a plunge into the blue, below freezing. It's a shock, and there I am, digging out the winter coats at 5 a.m., hoping to find them before the bus arrives.

What makes a character change, and how do we write that effectively into our novels without shocking the reader? How do we make it believable…and even more, accessible for our readers to do the same?

I have a little grid I use after I've laid down the story – think of it as a checklist – just to make sure I've gotten every element of change in the story:

| Act 1 | Act 2 | Act 3 |
|---|---|---|
| Glimpse of Hope<br>Invitation to change<br>Need to change | Attempt and failure<br>Cost consideration<br>Rewards<br>Desire<br>Attempt and mini-victory<br>Training for Battle | Black Moment<br>Epiphany<br>New Man (& Testing)<br>Happily Ever After |

As we go through each element, we'll stop and ask a Book Therapy question for you to apply to your book. When we finish, your character should have every step of the journey.

## Character Change: Glimpse of Hope

*These walls should be red!*

I have always longed for a red wall in my family room.

Yes, red. I saw one in a magazine, and then at a girlfriend's house, and I thought it would be a striking way to backdrop this incredible piece of Russian artwork I received from a friend. So, I sketched out the layout. I got paint samples. I compared them to the picture, and my other furniture. I found the right primer. I moved and covered furniture. Finally, I primed…and one beautiful morning, before the kids even left for school….I painted.

I love my red wall.

But it all started with a sense that my white walls weren't enough. Something was missing. I knew I wanted a pretty room – I just didn't know how to get there.

This is where your character starts. He has to start in a place of need, staring at white walls.

The first step is what I call the **Glimpse of Hope.**

As you open your story, your character has to lack something. A quality. A truth. An ability. Your character might not know they are missing something. But you, as the author, do—and you need to subtly communicate this to your reader..

Of course, you are starting your hero out on their journey in their home world. That's also going to be their "default" character, meaning their default beliefs and values. Something about these believes and values don't work, and they need to change.

In this first section, you want the character to do, see, be, or value something that indicates their need.

For example, in *Lord of the Rings: Fellowship of the Rings*, Frodo is amazed by his adventurous uncle Bilbo. He loves hearing about his stories, and is drawn to his bravery. Frodo isn't expressing his desire for adventure or courage – in fact, he doesn't even realize he has it. But we, the readers, see his desire in how he worships his uncle.

Let's take another of my favorite movies, *Eagle Eye*. The hero, Jerry Shaw is a whiz at poker, but is spending his life in a ho-hum job at a print shop. Even worse is that his twin brother is a hero of the country…something he believes he can never aspire to. We see his own inability to see himself as heroic after his brother's funeral, during an interaction with his father in his brother's room. With the trophies his brother earned as a backdrop, Jerry says that no, he's not going to try and re-enroll in college, and accepts his father's cutting remarks about his lack of drive. As the viewer, we despair with him, as he believes he'll never be anything more than a copy boy.

In *Cellular*, a fast paced thriller, our hero, Ryan, is a shallow, self-centered beach bum, who only agrees to help his girlfriend to win her affections. When he receives a phone call from a desperate woman who has been taken hostage, he has to be pressured by guilt into helping her. He can't even see how selfish he is, although he is offended that his girlfriend has accused him of this. Thankfully, he's agreed to help her in order to prove her wrong.

The key is to show your character's desire for something more, even if they can't believe it can be attained.

Here are some ideas for giving your reader that Glimpse of Hope:

1. Have your hero fail at doing something. Then have him—or someone else—comment that if only he had done or believed a certain way he might have accomplished his task. To which the hero says, "Well, that will never happen."

2. Have your hero, or just your reader, see something that the hero longs for – a happy family, a good job, a hero's welcome. Something that we can measure his later success by. I call it the glimpse of the **Happily Ever After.**

3. Have your hero hear of a story/legend/action that he wishes he could do.

**Book Therapy Question:**

    ✓  List your top five favorite movies, and watch the first ten minutes. Can you pinpoint the Glimpse of Hope -- that element that shows their desire for change?

    ✓  How can you show the reader what your character wants and the beliefs that hold them back from this in the first chapter? Insert this into your story.

## Character Change: Invitation to Change

*Release the Woobie!*

My son has a Woobie. You know, a security blanket? It's a disgusting denim comforter he sleeps with. It's ripped in seven places. The stuffing is coming out. If I wash it, it will disintegrate in my washer. I fear the Woobie.

So, while he was at school recently, well…I remade his bed. I washed his sheets. And I took the comforter and shoved it in a black plastic bag and hid it in the closet.

Hoping, maybe, he wouldn't…uh, notice?

He came home, and we all had a nice dinner and watched football and then…bedtime. I was reading, peacefully in my own bed when my son walked in with a distressed look.

"Mom, where is my….blanket?" Although fifteen, he bore the expression of a worried three year old, his voice shaking.

"Uh…." And here's where I tried to get creative. *"It's no longer with us."*

Fear flashed across his face. "It's not? Where is it?"

"Uh…Blankie Heaven?"

"Blankie Heaven!" His eyes widened and he swallowed hard. Looked outside. "It was garbage day today! You *didn't.*"

Now listen. *I did not lie.* I simply…shrugged. Made a little face, which one *might* have interpreted as an affirmative answer.

I had good intentions. I guess I was thinking I'd offer him a suitable alternative, one without the rips and the smells, and he'd take it like the man/football player he was.

Oh no.

He dropped to the floor (still in three-year-old mode) and shrieked, "Mommy, what have you done?"

Which brought in the other children, who, after my son declared my sins, were equally horrified at my actions. An hour later, after I'd exhausted *all* my psychological tactics (threats, shame, guilt, ridicule) I finally marched down to the closet and threw the plastic bag at him. He opened it like a starving man to C-rations.

"My blankie!" He clutched it to himself and then looked at me with an evil, very evil eye. "Do not touch my blankie again."

Oh, I'm not afraid. And this is *not* over. But I learned something.

I need to *prepare* my son for the surrender of his Woobie. I figure I have about three more years, after all…certainly he can't take it with him to college, right? Even if I had torn it from his clutches he would *still* need to go through the steps to *emotionally release it.*

You've started your character on their journey by giving your character a Glimpse of Hope. On the next step, you need to give them an **Invitation to Change.**

The Invitation is that moment when the character, very, very early on, is given the opportunity to do something different. To believe something, or value something, or try something that might change their lives. Often they turn it down, and it's that regret that drives them to have the opportunity again. For example, in *The Patriot*, there is a classic scene in the beginning where Benjamin Martin, the father, is talking with his peers who are deciding to go to war with Britain. He says that he's a father, and he doesn't have the luxury of living by his principles. The rest of the movie is about him regretting those words.

Sometimes, however, the characters will take the opportunity, and see how woefully under-equipped they are. Like, when Bilbo gives Frodo the ring. Frodo takes it (reluctantly) and has no idea what he's getting himself in for.

In *Cellular*, Ryan receives a call on the other line, and clicks over to take it. He is surprised that the kidnapped woman is still on the line…and he then allows her to talk him to the next stage in his journey.

The invitation to change is essential in building the rest of the journey of change. First, it creates a moment that the author can recreate later in the story as a "repeat" opportunity the character can then grab, showing their emotional change. It also sets up a concrete element that needs to change – a litmus test of sorts. For example, in *the Patriot*, Benjamin Martin is given an opportunity later to join up again. This time he takes it, showing that he's realized that his principles and his family are one. And Ryan, in *Cellular*, later loses the phone call – and has to fight to get it back, despite personal cost to himself.

In *Eagle Eye*, Jerry Shaw is told to run from his apartment…and fails to respond, thus is captured by the Feds. The next time this opportunity comes around….he listens and obeys.

The Invitation to Change also affords the character a moment to consider their missed opportunity, think about their vacancies either immediately or later, and builds in them the next component in their journey….the **Need to Change.**

**Book Therapy Question**

- ✓ Within the first three chapters, have you given your character an opportunity to believe or do something that they turn away from?

- ✓ Think ahead: How can you recast this choice into another moment later in the book?

# Character Change: Need to Change

*What is that Smell?*

I could see the problem. Actually, to be honest, I could smell it…seeping from my oldest son's tomb-like room, as if, yes, there might be a corpse inside. I stood at the threshold of the doorway and peered in. He lay, a lump under his sheets, the floor of his room riddled with the debris of his teenage boy existence – old pop cans, bowls of hardened ice cream, decaying socks, his grimy attire for the last week. All of it marinating in the brew of young manhood filth.

He needed to clean his room.

I flicked on the light (hey, it *was* 9 a.m.) "I think your room needs some attention."

Somewhere beneath the covers, he grunted.

"Seriously, I can't see your floor."

"It's there, or you'd be falling through to the center of the earth," mumbled the voice from the bed.

Oh, so cute. Ha ha.

"If you ever want to eat again, I'll see the floor of your room by dinnertime."

"I have to work. I won't be home for dinner."

I flicked off the light. Closed the door. Apparently, my external-maternal forces were no longer effective. I had to face the truth.

Change had to come from the inside.

And only when he recognized the need.

See, a character isn't going to change unless properly motivated. They might see a Glimmer of Hope, and even be invited by circumstances to change, but without seeing the need they won't have the strength to tackle the challenges (or, in my son's case, the smells).

The Invitation to Change, whether they accept it or not, needs to be followed, in short order, by, the Need to Change.

Remember the scene in *Lord of the Rings: Fellowship of the Rings* when Frodo and gang are hiding in the woods as the creepy Nasgould are looking for them? Suddenly, for the first time, Frodo realizes the danger they are in. He doesn't fully comprehend it, but they're terrifying enough that he knows it's serious.

And, he knows he's going to have to do something about it. What, he's not sure, but the need is compelling enough to make him try.

In *The Patriot*, after Benjamin Martin safely secures his children at his sister-in-law's plantation, he realizes that he has been wrong not to get involved in the war – it came to him anyway. He realizes that he hasn't protected his family by trying to stay neutral – there is no neutrality in this war, and they would be drawn into the war against their will. So…the only way to protect his family is to help drive the British from the land.

In *Eagle Eye*, Jerry Shaw is arrested and at the mercy of the NSA, accused of a crime he didn't commit but is clearly being framed for. It's apparent that the NSA doesn't believe him. Thus, if he doesn't take matters into his own hands and figure out who is framing him, he'll end up behind bars.

The Need to Change is embodied in an early event or situation that should be strong and terrible enough to convince your character to grab the opportunity to change the next time it might rear its head. And, it must be a sufficient enough threat that it will force him to confront his demons and fears, or beliefs – all those obstacles that will stand in the way to change.

Because if he doesn't have to change, well then you're just going to have to close the door and wait until he's disgusted by his own horrible smell. And really, who knows how long that might take?

**Book Therapy Questions:**

- ✓ What situation, threat, loss, reward or fear would be strong enough to make your character want to change?

- ✓ How can you raise that need so that it looms over your character and they can't escape it?

Now, you are at the end of the first act of your story – you've shown your character's Glimpse of Hope, ideally during his Home World, and chapter one. Then, you've given them an Invitation to Change – something they've turned down, and which has led to their regret. Finally, you've created a situation that shows their Need to Change because to stay in their own emotional mess, they're doomed.

If you were to put this into the Book Therapy Plotting Roadmap, you would plot the emotional journey alongside the Plot:

Home World/Glimpse of Hope

Inciting Incident/Invitation to Change

  The Big Debate....Regret of the Missed Opportunity

Need to Change...which results in The Noble Quest

Okay, now take a breath and if you want, just go ahead put your ideas on paper. Use the chart below to plug in the answers to your Book Therapy questions, making sure you've started your character correctly on his emotional journey. Don't worry, you'll have a chance to incorporate it into the full story plot in the appendix of the book.

Or, simply continue on to Act 2.

| Plot | Emotional Journey |
|---|---|
| **ACT 1** | |
| Life/Distancing | Glimpse of Hope |
| Inciting Incident | Invitation to Change |
| The Big Debate/Regret of Missed Opportunity | |
| Need to Change/Noble Quest | |

So now your character sees his Need for Change, and is fueled by the regret of missing it the first time, as well as a glimpse of what it might look like. Let's allow him to give it a shot.

### Act 2: First down and 10!

I love football. Hometown high school, college ball, and pro, in that order. I am a fan of *Friday Night Lights*, and every football movie made (well, almost...I'm not into the spoofy football movies – it's much too serious a sport for that!) and most of all, football players!

I married a football player. I like them because when they get hit, they get back up. (Probably why I like bullriders too.). Does it hurt? Yes. But they shake it off, line up and try again. They get four downs to get it right.

Our local football team took a hard hit on a recent Friday night, losing for the first time in 16 games, in the last 45 seconds. But I had to give props to both teams...they didn't stop fighting until the last second.

The Second Act, and subsequent steps of character change, are much like the ten yard run/four downs of a football game.

**Attempt (and failure)**
**Cost consideration**
**Rewards**
**Desire**
**Attempt and mini-victory**
**Training for Battle**

Let's take a closer look at the football metaphor: The offense has the ball, they need to make their ten yards, and they line up, and run the first play. Maybe the drop back for a pass, and our hero, the Quarterback (QB), is sacked. Worse, he's injured.

Now they huddle up. Obviously, the defenders have heard about their amazing passing game, so they'll have to try a different tact. But their superstar fullback is also out of the game with a mean cold, thanks to this Minnesota weather, so the tailback might not get the blocking he needs for the sweet play. If the QB steps in to block, he might get further injured by the rather large senior playing on defense. However, they are on the twenty yard line, and six points down, with a minute left on the board. And, they are second in the state, if they can win this game.

So, they run the sweep, and sure enough they get the first down. But the QB is taken out, which opens the door for the Third Act when our hero, the QB, has to decide if he's really the hero everyone is counting on....

Maybe that is too much football, so let's break it down.

## Character change: Attempt and Failure

The next stage in the journey is the attempt by the hero to go after the prize, to rescue the fair maiden, or stand up to the bully, or face his fears. His attempts not only fail, but sometimes make everything worse!

Remember when Frodo is enticed to surrender the ring to Galadriel, the Noldorin princess? For the first time, he realizes that he is not quite strong enough to bear this burden, if even she can't. It frightens him, and he's overwhelmed with the task.

For example, going back to the football metaphor – the defense just can't stop the offense, despite the fact they keep getting beat up, and are blitzing to the best of their abilities. The problem is the offense knows their holes. Th solution – the epiphany, usually figured out during half-time! – is to run a different defense and call some audibles (change the play on the line).

In other words, all the plays your character is making don't work – their attempts to solve the problem only creates new ones.

So…now that your character sees his need to change, give them the opportunity to try. Fight the dragon, reach out to a husband, attack the enemy….and fail. And, if you can, make it worse.

In *The Patriot*, Benjamin Martin's band of militia start winning against the British…and earn their wrath, thus causing the British to begin killing the families of the militia.

In *Eagle Eye*, when Jerry Shaw decides that he isn't going to obey the voice on the other end of the telephone, he is exposed in a subway of commuters as a terrorist.

So…have them attempt to change…and fail miserably. Then you'll be in a place to draw him back to the huddle to consider the costs.

**Book Therapist Question**

✓ What attempts could your character do to change…and how can you make them fail?

✓ Now…make that failure worse by creating a new problem.

## Character Change: Cost Consideration

*What's it going to cost me?*

Ever been on a diet over Christmas season? I have a Russian friend who is a pilot, and his annual exam arrives *right* after New Year's Eve. He gets his blood drawn and his cholesterol checked…it's a bummer, because in order to keep his pilot's license, he has to pass a certain level.

Which means he has to diet over Christmas.

He has to stay away from rich foods and, of course wine, which is big in Russia during New Year's Eve. He stands at the pinnacle of the season, smells the holiday feast, and I know he laments his life. (Or at least the timing of his exam.)

But in order to be a pilot, he has to surrender something.

So does your character. Right after he or she fails their first attempt, they'll have to regroup, and take a good look at their weaknesses and vacancies, and realize the truth: If they want victory, they can't stay the way they are.

Another way to put it: Anything worth fighting for is going to cost something.

Some "considering the cost" moments from my favorite movies:

When Frodo takes off across the boat at the end of *Lord of the Rings: the Fellowship of the Rings*, and Samwise nearly dies going after him. Frodo realizes that his quest *will* cost lives, and that he has to be brave enough to let that happen.

In *The Princess Bride*, remember the moment right after Wesley and Buttercup get through the fire swamp, and evil king Humperdink finds them? Buttercup negotiates Wesley's release but surrenders herself to be married to the king, believing that her man will get killed if she doesn't. (She later learns that she must believe that death will not stop true love!)

How about *You've Got Mail?* Remember the scene where the hero and heroine are going to meet in the coffee shop for the first time – but the hero sees her and realizes that ShopGirl is his nemesis! He'll have to regroup and win her heart online before he can reveal himself. He sacrifices the opportunity to meet her in the hopes that something better will transpire.

Going back to some of the movies we've talked about:

In *Cellular*, Ryan is running up the stairs in the police station with the cell phone when the reception begins to fail. Worse, on the other end of the line, the victim is attacked and we discover her child is in jeopardy. Suddenly our hero has to make a choice: Will he alert the police, and possibly let the reception die, or will he attempt to save the child before the villains can kidnap him, also? His cost? He won't be able to complete the errand for his girlfriend, thus confirming his irresponsibility (in her eyes) and losing the girl.

Give your hero a moment to consider what character change will cost him – and have it be brutal, something that is a true sacrifice. Only then will the sacrifice be truly heart-wrenching.

## Book Therapist Question

- ✓ What does your character have to lose if he tries again, or continues on the quest?

- ✓ Have you created enough of a motivation to sacrifice their dream despite the pain? (ie, losing something *greater?*)

## Character change: Rewards

*Yeah, but what about me?*

So, every summer, I take the five week beginner's tennis class through our local community center. Let me say that again. *Every summer I take the beginner's tennis class.*

That's right. Just the *beginner's*. Yes, there's an intermediate class. And an advanced level class. And then people actually *play* each other. For points. And wins.

But see, progressing would require something, well, that I've tried to push out of my brain ever since I escaped six years of piano lessons: practice.

Now the thing is, I do like tennis. I like watching it and I like playing it. I like hitting the ball so that it bounces inside the line, and then out of reach of my opponent. Yes, occasionally it happens. But for the most part, there I am, the one hitting air as the ball flies past me.

It's gonna take a lot of practice to get this girl into the intermediate class. And truth is: I just don't see it. Because once I get there – I'm going to have to play *other* intermediate players. Who will beat me. And then I'll have to practice more to get to the *advanced* level. Where I'll get beat again.

The bottom line is…why? What's in it for me? (Humiliation is not a reward, by the way.) I suppose someone could suggest that I could concentrate on the *fun* of tennis – and it is fun – and the occasional thrill when I land a serve *inside* the service box. But so far, the reward isn't greater than the cost.

(Although, something inside me compels to return to the courts every summer. I think that's called *faith*.)

Now that you've brought your character to their first attempt and failure, and given them a glimpse of what it will cost them to succeed, then you need to give them a reward for succeeding.

Your character has to see past the **Costs** to the **Rewards**. And, they have to believe that it's possible. Or at least, that it could be. Seeing the Costs and the Rewards will make them look inside, to ask *why* that Reward is worth fighting for. (Later, they'll discover what it is inside them that stands in the way.) But for now they have to believe that their attempt and cost is worth the battle.

So, how do you give them a reward? Here are some ideas:

1. **Give them a hero.** Someone who has been the course, and fought the good fight, who knows the Reward. Like Jean Villeneuve, the French Commander who befriends Benjamin Martin, who has lost his daughters and wife to the British, but has fought with honor. And, Gabriel, Benjamin's oldest son who fights with compassion. He believes that others have kept their character and goodness intact…perhaps he can also. Other heroes are Obe-Wan-Kenobi, who was the Jedi master, and Luke's mentor. Or, in *Sleepless in Seattle*, Annie's parents, who had a long-lasting true love.

2. **Give them a glimpse of the darkness.** Up the ante by adding into the mix the "what if we do nothing" question. Give them a glimpse of what could happen if they *don't* fight the good fight. For, example, at the end of *Lord of the Rings: the Fellowship of the Ring*, Frodo and gang fight Mordor's creepy army, and they realize just how evil Sauron is. They know their destruction will overrun the land if they don't stop it.

3. **Give them a cause.** Kidnap their sidekick, make them fall in love with the princess, save a kingdom – anything to make them realize that if they give up, they'll lose what they love. *Titanic* is a classic example (I can't think of that movie without hearing – "Jack, Jack! Come back!") Falling in love makes them realize what they have to live for! In *Eagle Eye*, Jerry Shaw is bound by honor – the life of the son of the woman whose fate is tied with his is at risk.

The Reward has to be at least as vivid, as compelling, as tangible as the cost. Or frankly, they'll end up taking the beginner's class, year after year, after year.

**Book Therapy Question**

&#x2713; Have you given your character a glimpse of the reward that awaits change, and victory?
      Giving them a Hero?
      Showing them the alternative?
      Giving them another cause to fight for?

## Character Change: Creating Desire

(from the Caldron of Cost and Reward)

*What do you really want?*

How much are you willing to pay for your freedom? To achieve a goal or dream? To save a loved one? To win love?

Every story we write has an arch, a journey, driven by the protagonist. But what drives the protagonist?

What is he or she after? Why? Does the reward justify the cost? In other words, why is it worth it?

When you put the cost against the reward, and stir it together, you discover the crux of the heroes' journey…their true desire.

In *Braveheart*, William Wallace considers the cost of war and the lives of Scotland's men worth the reward of freedom. But when he looks deeper in his heart, he's fighting for justice and to avenge the death of his wife.

We talk a lot about "Why?" in My Book Therapy. Why does the character want to do this or that, why is it worth the fight, the loss?

At some point in the huddle the characters are going to say, "Why are we doing this? Sure, we see a state title within our grasp, and we're angry that our quarterback has just been sidelined by a late hit and we're playing the team that beat us last year in the finals—but why?"

This is where true change begins to take place. It's not about the fears or rewards…it's about the people they want to be. When a character looks inward and asks, "What do I truly desire?" then we see true change.

Honor. Our football players are fighting for honor. For Manhood.

In *Eagle Eye,* Jerry Shaw has just about had it…and he isn't going to go a step further until…he finds out the son of the woman is in jeopardy. And, that his brother wasn't a traitor…that in fact, he was a hero. And Jerry is given the chance to be a hero, too, if he'll stay the course. So, Jerry looks at the cost – losing his ho-hum life (and perhaps his life) and the reward (saving his country) and it requires him to ask…what does he really want?

He wants to be a hero, like his brother.

It's as simple as…when your character comes back to the huddle, asking…what do you really want?

In a lot in the manuscripts I read, the answer is…Love. He wants to find love.

Well, that's noble and universal, but why? Finding true love is a noble journey, but will not make for a very interesting book. How much does he want true love? Why is true love important?

Let's say our hero, let's call him, Dragonslayer the Third, wakes up one morning, sees a beautiful day and says to his Man-in-Waiting, "Alfred, today I want to find true love."

Well, off we go. He spies his first Beautiful Damsel. He approaches. "You, there, gorgeous woman so fair. Hark, and come with me. I want to love you and make you my Queen."

"What? Fergetabboutit. You're too pretty for me."

Dragon turns to Alfred, "She turned me down. How rude!"

"My Lord, she must be a twit."

"Certainly, well, it's lunch. Shall we dine? And what fun shall I have for tomorrow?"

Dragonslayer has no reason to pursue true love the moment he faced his first obstacle. He needs a reason, and hopefully something beyond 1, True love is grand or 2. His mother abandoned him as a baby.

If you're having trouble figuring out what your character truly wants, try this:

What was the one moment in his life that he was truly happy? (In *Eagle Eye*, we actually see a glimpse of this in Jerry's memory, when he's playing baseball with his brother, and he clearly adores him). Usually this moment reflects something of what your character truly desires. It's this desire that is at the root of his motivation.

In the movie *Titanic*, Rose wants true love but she also wants freedom from her mother, from societal expectations. When she meets Jack, she discovers the courage to change her dreams. We see that this is her desire when she has the courage to stand on the bow, let Jack hold her, and she says that she is flying.

What about Lucy in *While You Were Sleeping?* She falls in love with Jack, the other brother. But the family she's fallen in love with wants her to marry the responsible older brother Peter. If she confesses her feelings, the cost is almost too great. She'll lose this wonderful family because she lied. She'll lose the man she loves. But her happiest moments is when her father and her dreamed of going amazing places. She wants a man who will give her the world, not security.

Getting to the bottom of your character's desire is the first step in creating true character change.

**Book Therapist Question:**

&check;  What is your character's happiest memory?

&check;  What about that memory would he like to recreate or hold on to?

&check;  How can you turn that memory into his greatest desire?

&check;  How does that motivate him to pick himself back up and dive back into the fight?

## Character Change: Attempt and Mini-Victory

*Once is not enough!*

So far, we've covered our hero's goal and desire, he's calculated cost versus reward and he's attempted to achieve his goal. And failed. Hopefully, miserably!

Now, we have to let him win. Something. One game. One touchdown. One completed pass. Enough for our character to feel like they've accomplished something.

My husband and I recently learned to swing dance. For a guy who claims he has no rhythm, he does a great job keeping the beat and leading me around the dance floor. I tried to tell him this, but alas, he couldn't hear it.

Still, because he wanted to make me happy, he decided to take us dancing at a local venue's '50's night. After three songs I managed to coax him to the dance floor. He stayed in the basic step for about fifteen measures…then led me in a turn. Then another. Then another. The dance ended with him smiling. "Hey, I did it!"

Yes. The victory was enough to convince him to stay on the floor for the rest of the night, and later earn the esteem of a couple ladies who commented on what a great dancer he was! (Another taste of victory!)

In *Eagle Eye*, Jerry Shaw experiences the taste heroism as he evades his captors - of course under the direction of the computer that continues to call him – still, with each heroic step he's forced to take, he experiences a taste of the person he wants to become.

In *The Patriot*, Benjamin Martin is victorious against the British – even outwitting them in their own fort, and causing the General's Great Danes to love him. His tactics, although brutal, are winning the war.

The Attempt and Mini-Victory happens early on the in the Second Act – early enough to leave room for what is called…**Training for Battle.**

## Character change: Training for Battle

Or, what I call...the fun and games.

Your character isn't going to literally "train for battle" – but rather, be put through a number of tests. Interpersonal challenges. Physical foibles. Through which, we'll see him have to look inside and make changes.

*You've Got Mail* is a great example of this "Training for Battle" concept. Remember when our hero is about to meet Meg for the first time in the coffee shop, and he realizes that it's his nemesis form the "shop around the corner?" (We discussed this scene in the Cost portion of the journey.) He then tells her in the next scene that he has a project that will need some "tweaking" before they can get together.

The next forty-five minutes or so of the movie are about that tweaking. He proceeds to "woo" her because he's realized that once she finds out who he is, she'll hate him. So, he must make her fall in love with him in the flesh, so that she won't reject him as her online friend.

This is the guts of the book. And the part of the story that is most easily mis-plotted. We'll get to how to plot this portion in section two, but for now, follow these principles:

1. Every obstacle your character faces must make the journey more difficult, causing them to dig deeper and find a character trait that they didn't have before.
2. They will get "better" at the skills they are developing – whether it be better at completing the tasks the computer tells them to do (*Eagle Eye*), or better at keeping the cell reception and finding the bad guys (*Cellular*), or better at fighting battles (*The Patriot*), or better winning football games, or better at winning the heart of the heroine.
3. Each time they get better, they become more the person they hope to be, a bigger glimpse of hope...So, give them a glimpse of something they long for. Let them kiss the girl, win the division championship, outwit the bad guys, or figure out why the computer wants to destroy the world.

Sure, your character will have some failures during this section. Some slammed doors, maybe some cuts and bruises, but eventually, they will grow stronger, wiser, more handsome.

Eventually, they're going to feel so empowered that they think they're on top of the world, they've solved the problem, they're on their way to sure victory...

Then, you're going to rip the rug from under them, and push them right into their black moment.

In my recent book *Nothing But Trouble*, my character, a wanna-be PI struggles with jumping to conclusions that lead her down rabbit trails. But, during this "growth" phase, I have her get a

number of things right, and use her sleuthing skills well, until she thinks she's practically Sherlock Holmes.

Of course, that's when the *real* bad guy shows up.

During the Training for Battle Stage, I recommend having 3-4 big events, either physical or emotional, that challenge them. If you have my book *From the Inside…Out: discover, create and publish the novel in you!*, then you know I recommend a process called **The D's** to plot this portion – I call them **Disappointments** – but they could get progressively worse: (Here's my plug for Brandilyn Collins' book, *Getting into Character*, the first person to use the D's for plotting)

**Disappointment**
**Disaster**
**Destruction**
**Devastation**

Think like this: For every victory, your character must have a loss…something that makes it worse. Perhaps, they leave a trail for the villain to find them, or the they are setting themselves up to have their heart broken, or perhaps they are getting deeper into a lie…whatever the case may be, you want to find situations that lead them to a place where there is no turning back, and no hope.

We'll talk more about plotting in the **Plotting** section of the book, but for now, begin jotting down ideas of how to train your characters for battle.


**Book Therapist Question:**

- ✓ Ask yourself going into each scene during this section –

    - o What losses can they have?

    - o What victories?

    - o What does my character learn in this scene that makes him/her a stronger/better person?
- ✓ How do you give them another glimpse of hope, this time in themselves?

| ACT 2 | |
|---|---|
| Attempt | Failure |
| Cost consideration | Rewards |
| Desire | |

| Attempt and Mini-Victory | |
| --- | --- |
| **Training for Battle** | |
| Disappointment | What do they learn? |
| Disaster | What do they learn? |
| Destruction | What do they learn? |
| Devastation | |

## Act 3: It's all about the change!

### Character Change: The Black Moment

It was after midnight, on some turnpike south of Pittsburg when my husband declared he wanted to set our house on fire.

Of course, our "house" was a twenty-eight foot motor home that we lived in as we traveled around the United States during furlough as we raised support to head out on our second term on the mission field in Russia. We had just spent six days living in a tent in a campground while a repair shop fixed it. We'd also spent our last six hundred dollars.

And fifty miles down the road, with the kids sleeping in the bunks in back, the motor home started to smoke. We drifted to the side of the road. Got out, and as my husband stared at the cracked head gasket, he said, "Do you think the insurance will figure it out if I set it on fire?"

Black moment. It's when life feels overwhelming, when your character's worst fears come true, when things can't get any worse.

When Frodo succumbs to the ring in Mt. Mordor.

When Gabriel dies in Benjamin's arms.

When the Titanic goes down.

When Jerry Shaw realizes he's going to be the villain instead of the hero.

When your character realizes that everything they've tried to do has failed, and that they can't ever be the person, or have the dream they longed for.

If you started with *From the Inside…Out: discover, create and publish the novel in you*, then you know that when you develop your characters, you discover their greatest fears, and why they had them, and then used them to create the Black Moment. Every character's Black Moment will be different, uniquely crafted to suit them and bring them to their lowest place.

*Why is this Black Moment so important?* Because we want them to examine *why* this is their lowest place, and confront the beliefs, even perhaps a spiritual lie that has pushed them through life to this dark place. Or maybe, they just need to accept the situation, and figure out how to go forward.

Nevertheless, as they sit in this darkness, they'll need to search for truth, the *light* so to speak. They'll be looking for an epiphany....which is the next stage of character growth. The epiphany should be a truth, a realization, and something that touches the core of their beliefs and changes them.

The key here is to create a Black Moment that assaults their values...what they believe about themselves.

For example, in my upcoming book *Nothing But Trouble*, PJ Sugar believes that she is faulty, that she just can't help but get into trouble. And, I confirm that in her Black Moment by accusing her of a crime she didn't commit, although all signs point to her guilt. Not only that, but because of her actions, her nephew's life is in danger, and the man she loves believes that she is guilty. She realizes that she has to stop believing she is flawed, and start living in the truth – that she's exactly who she should be, and spiritually, God delights in her, despite her cracks. She has an entire paradigm shift, which allows her to see herself and the world differently.

My Book Therapy partner Rachel Hauck recently wrote a book called *The Sweet By and By*. Her character Jade has to realize that a choice she made as a teen has tainted her life since, was *her* choice. Not her mother's or other pressures, but her. She feels if she admits it she has betrayed her last port of call, her last safe haven. It's not easy to turn on yourself. But she cannot move on with her life without facing her sin.

The Black Moment is a combination of a repeat (in some way) of this darkest moment, and the lie becoming so huge it feels overwhelming.

For example, Jerry Shaw, based on his childhood memories with his brother, believes that he can never measure up. And he's lived his life based on this lie. In his darkest moment, he believes that not only will he not measure up to his brother, the hero, but he, in fact, will become the most hated man in America, an assassin.

In *The Patriot*, Benjamin Martin believes that there is no honor in war, and that the sins of his past (when he committed a brutal crime in the French-American war) would repay him in some way. When Gabriel, his oldest son, dies (the second of his sons to die), he believe this lie to be true.

Of course, in *Lord of the Rings: The Fellowship of the Ring*, the lie is that Frodo can overcome the power of the ring. And the Black Moment is when he rips it from his neck and puts it on his finger...and then gets his finger bit off, only to leave him dangling off the cliff, ready to be lost forever.

In short: You want to devastate your character and bring them to their knees. A Black Moment has to come out of the character's journey. Make it sincere to your character and the story. Don't come up with a Black Moment so dark it doesn't resonate with your character. Hence, the key to finding your character's black moment is to ask the following questions:

**Book Therapist Question:**

- ✓ What is the darkest moment in your character's past – something that has changed them as a person?

- ✓ What did they learn from this dark moment?

- ✓ What lie do they believe as a result of that event, and how has this affected their life?

## Character Change: Epiphany

We have a Christmas tradition in our family that we started when the children were young. We do a jigsaw puzzle every holiday season. We started with a 30 piece puzzle. Now that the kids are teenagers and adults we do 2000 piece puzzles. It's a great feeling to put a puzzle together, to complete a section and see it come to life. But the best, the triumphant moment is hunting for a piece for hours, trying thousands...only to finally discover the right one. One of our sons has an "Aha!" dance he does, another taps the piece, making sure everyone knows of their triumph.

And when that piece completes a picture, it's even more satisfying.

The **Epiphany** is the missing piece of the puzzle. It's that recognition of some faulty belief or wrong action that has handicapped your character and then the realization of what I call the **Truth that sets them Free.**

For Jerry Shaw, it's the recognition that his brother trusted him all along, and the realization that being a Hero just means doing the right thing.

For Benjamin Martin, it's the recognition that Gabriel knew what he was fighting for – freedom – and never surrendered his honor (embodied in the flag he was sewing). He realizes that yes, he can fight with honor on the battlefield.

In *Cellular,* Ryan recognizes that he no longer cares what his former girlfriend thinks of him. And it's the realization that he is responsible – enough to save the heroine's life.

In *Titanic,* it's the recognition that Rose has survived, and the realization that she can live differently, free of who she is "supposed" to be, even without Jack.

In *You've Got Mail,* it's the recognition by Kathleen Kelly she has forgiven Joe Fox, despite the crimes he's perpetrated by closing her store, and the realization that she wishes he might be the man on the other end of the computer.

How do you find the Epiphany Truth?

Go back to the construction of the Black Moment and ask specific questions.

**Book Therapist Question:**

- ✓ What can they look past and recognize?
- ✓ What can they look forward and realize? (Or…what Truth sets them free?)

## Character Change: He's a New Man!

*What do I do now?*

So, now that our hero has confronted his Darkest Moment and seen the light, we've come to the last step of character change: The **New Man**. The changed person he/she has become, complete with new skills, new beliefs, and new courage.

For example, remember the scene in *The Hunt for Red October* where, after they're on the submarine, and *after* Sean Connery says (in his terrible Russian, I might add), to Jack Ryan "Oh, I remember you – you wrote that book, and got it all wrong" – Jack has a mini-Black Moment there. A realization that he's not all right. And, although he doesn't do a lot of soul searching (because it's a high action flick), we do see him shaken.

He has to confront the belief that he doesn't know everything. That he can be wrong….but that it will still turn out okay. And then he *tests* this belief by going with the Russian captain to who is on a mission to shoot his own man. (which, militarily, makes no sense), while the *American* captain is forced to keep the sub from being blown up. (Again…making no sense). *But*, it does make sense within our character change grid. Instead of following his logic, which Jack Ryan must do, he has to trust his future to faith. To *hoping* he got it right, and trusting that everything will work out.

Or how about *Independence Day?* Remember the Black Moment in the aliens' Mother Ship, when our heroes can't disengage and fly away after uploading the virus? They realize that they have to sacrifice their lives, and that it's worth it. (Something that the scientist, David Levinson (play by Jeff Goldblum) wasn't ready to do at the beginning of the movie). Only *then* are they willing to shoot off the nuclear rocket, and then race for their lives out of the ship (against all odds).

In some way, we need to see that our character is a **New Man**….and the best way to do this is to test him by making him fight for the truth through: **Final Battle, Loss, Reminder, Victory.**

The **Final Battle** is the final challenge they must face. Storming the castle, running after the girl, facing the villain…whatever they've been preparing for the entire book.

The **Loss** represents an obstacle in the way, some derailment of their quest – from a defeat to a death, but some element of loss. It can also occur when the "lie" attacks him a final time.

The **Reminder** is just that – a reminder of his Epiphany, the truth that has set him free, reminding him that he is a New Man. Your character grasps this Epiphany, this truth, and holds on for dear life, making it a part of him.

Finally, the **Victory** is the New Man changed, the accomplishment of his goals, and the happy ending.

I like to use *The Patriot* because it is an actual battle, but that is the metaphor for the ending section of a story. See, armed with the *truth*, your New Man will face their last challenge. In that last challenge, they'll come face to face with their former beliefs, or the lie, falter, and then forge ahead in victory.

In *The Patriot*, Martin's militia is asked to fight on the line – fight honorably, and they rise to the challenge. But, as the battle ensues, they falter and begin to retreat. Martin, meanwhile, has in his sights Tavington – the man who killed both his sons. He is running forward to kill him when he realizes that his men are fleeing. So, he has to make a choice – does he go after Tavington, embracing revenge or help his men stay in the fight? The loss is the opportunity to face Tavington…but also the loss of the honor of his men. (and, the "lie" raises its ugly head)

Martin turns around and sees his men running and, in a very metaphorical moment, he throws down his weapon and grabs a flag (the truth!) Then he turns and calls his men back to action – choosing honor over revenge.

The Patriots surge over the hill, then of course, Benjamin is free to fight Tavington, having defeated the belief that he can't fight honorably, and realizing he can choose honor over the bloodthirsty man he'd been.

In *Eagle Eye*, Jerry Shaw, dressed as a guard, breaks into the Senate chambers, intent on saving the life of the President. He realizes that he is powerless – the bomb is about to go off. In the final battle, he makes the choice to run into the fray, shouting. He looks around and realizes that he has to play the part of assassin in order to stop the attack, losing his honor and seeing the lie that he will never be a hero. But the reminder is that he knows that indeed, he's a hero, someone just like his brother. So he climbs up on the desk, closes his eyes, (holding onto the truth!) and fires the gun over his head. And, he earns a barrage of bullets.
    But Jerry Shaw has saved the life of the president, and the heroine's son. Victory.

After your epiphany, *test* your New Man. Give him an opportunity to be the person he's longed to be…and your reader will cheer.

And it doesn't hurt to let your hero get the girl in the end. It makes for the **Happily Ever After** we all long for.

Now, let's build these last elements into our plot.

| ACT 3 | |
|---|---|
| Devastation/Black Moment | |
| Epiphany/Aha! Truth that sets them free! | |
| New Man/Final Battle | |
| Loss/Lie | |

**Book Therapist Question:**
- ✓ Do you have a New Man moment in your story?
- ✓ How can you build in the final battle, loss, reminder and victory into your finale?

| Reminder/Hold onto the truth |
| --- |
| |

| Victory! |
| --- |
| |

| Happily Ever After ending |
| --- |
| |

So....there you have it, the process of character change for your character.

But how, you say, do you get your reader to fall in love with your character and believe in that change?

You have to make him reveal his heart....or, peel back his layers.

## Part Two: Revealing your character for greatest emotional impact.

You've plotted your character's emotional journey. Now how do you translate him or her onto the page without making feel like a plastic or cardboard cutout? How do you make a reader see your character as you do? How do you make your character come to life so that your reader cries with him, falls in loves with him, rejoices with him?

Remember the last time you fell in love? You saw him or her across the room, and something about their physical appearance intrigued you. It told you something about them – perhaps they were brave, or strong, or creative, or disheveled, or rough-edged. You probably noticed their mannerisms, maybe how they talked, how they smiled, how they handled themselves. Even before you met, their clothing and demeanor gave you a general impression about them.

Then you met them. You found out their name, where they were from. You saw how they treated the waitress, or the hotel clerk, or an employee. Perhaps you saw their habits, their music, their tastes in décor, their car. Hopefully, you also saw how they reacted to situations of joy, or stress. This gave you a hint about their internal character, what they were good at, even hinted at their values.

After a first date, you might have discovered their life goals, and perhaps what he or she wants most right now. You maybe have talked about your childhood, or your dreams, and what struggles you have in finding them. You may have gotten a glimpse at a major event that shaped their lives. All of this revealed their purpose in life, the Noble Cause that drove them to make the choices they made.

After a few dates, perhaps you had a first fight. He or she reacted to that fear of getting hurt. In that moment, you saw their history with love, maybe even a hint at their deepest fears, making you think back to the events that shaped them. Suddenly you felt as if you looked inside their hearts, and if your fight made you a stronger couple, then it made your heart more tender toward him or her as you understood their insecurities and perhaps embraced their dreams.

Finally, you came to the place where you knew you had to go forward or break up. You came to that barrier between dating and true love, and if he struggled to cross it, you saw his darkest fears and his spiritual lies that kept him from finding happiness. Hopefully he or she broke through the barrier with an epiphany or truth that gave them the courage to declare their love. Ahh….I love falling in love. Seeing the heart of someone else, and embracing it.

And your reader does, too.

*The First key to deeper characterization is a technique called Character layering.*

## Character layering

Character Layering is all about slowly revealing the heart of your character – to your other characters in the story and, ultimately, to your reader.

But doesn't my reader need to know about my character in order to love them?

No.

Think back – if you knew everything about your spouse or significant other when you met them, would you still go forward? Perhaps it's best if we fall in love layer by layer.

More than that, your reader wants to dive into the story, and too much too soon just bogs it down. If you dump your hero's entire bio onto the page, not only will it seem forced, but it also will lack impact. The fun of getting to know a character is discovering who they are and what makes them tic. The best part of a book is discovering the **Dark Secret**, or desperate motivation behind their actions. If you reveal it all at once it lacks punch, and you've stolen the emotional impact of the story from the reader.

Character Layering solves the problem of what to tell, when.

The reason we see huge chunks of **Backstory** in a novel is because the author is trying to figure out their own character. They're getting into their character's skin and working through his layers to figure out his behavior. This is perfectly acceptable….for a rough draft. Go ahead and put on your character. Take as many pages as you need and then … cut it. Put it in a "Character" file and *then* start your story.

But I'm getting ahead of myself. Before you can unlayer your character, or even start your story, you have to build your character.

And that means….Backstory.

## Building Backstory

It is essential to know the Backstory of your character *before* you start the book because as I mentioned, you want to start your story quickly, without too much bio. But you need to understand your character because it's their Backstory that causes them to react in present. The reader just needs to see the *outcome* of the Backstory, and how it affected your character.

**So, how much Backstory should you develop?**

*Answer: Enough to know your characters motivations for why he/she does the things they do in your story.*

If your character loved to draw as a child and always dreamed of being an artist, that's only important if it has something to do with the plot. If he's a detective solving a murder, it might not have anything to do with the story. However, if he is asked to draw the suspect and rediscovers the rusty talent he had, then perhaps it is slightly important. If, even better, he loved to draw, and had talent, but his father told him he was a terrible artist (in order to discourage such a "frivolous" career), and the story is about a policeman who discovers that he has the ability to see the crimes in the pictures he draws, (and thus was always meant to use this God-given gift) well, suddenly this Backstory takes on relevance.

As the author, you always want to figure out what elements of their past molded them into the people they are today. Mostly because you're going to use the fears and dreams, the secrets and mistakes from their past to construct their story, and to help your reader fall in love with your character.

I've read countless books where the character seems to have been born on page one. They're flat, uninteresting, even unbelievable. Even worse, however, is when the character's entire life history is fleshed out in the first three chapters. I'm not going to remember (as a reader) what college he/she went to. But tell me that he witnessed a murder as a ten year old, and yes, that I'll remember.

If you've read *From the Inside-Out: discover, create and publish the novel in you*, you know that I am a proponent of sitting your character down and chatting with him about why he is who he is. This is how you discover the Backstory, and is essential for a well-rounded, three-dimensional, living breathing character, and the key to creating a hero/heroine that your reader will root for.

So, what questions do you ask to discover their Backstory?

## Developing the Backstory

If you've taken any of my classes, read the My Book Therapy blog, or read *From the Inside-Out*, you know I like to use the Five Elements of Self-Esteem as a foundation for plotting and character development.

I also like to use them for building the elements of layering.

For a more in-depth explanation of the Five Elements of Self-Esteem and how to build them into a plot, check out *From the Inside-Out*. (This is available through the My Book Therapy store, or at Amazon.com)

The Five Elements of Self-Esteem help us determine who our character is, why they do the things they do, what their greatest fears and dreams are, how to make them suffer, how to craft the Black Moment, their perfect Epiphany, and finally the happily ever after ending.

They will also help us layer our character, step by step.

What are the components of our character's layers?

1. **Identity:** Everyone has an identity they use to introduce themselves to others. The first layer reflects how they see themselves, or how the world sees them.

When you meet someone for the first time, you are basing your impressions on who they are by how they dress, what they are doing at the time, perhaps the speech they use, and the way they introduce themselves. This gives us the first glimpse as to who they are. So, who is your character? What identity does he give himself? What external trappings go along with that identity?

What impression do they give to the world because of that identity?

For example from my book *Happily Ever After,* my hero Joe, considers himself a drifter, and when he meets the heroine, Mona for the first time, he looks like one – a wreck of a truck, a duffle bag, a mangy dog, faded jeans, workboots, a flannel shirt, a scruffy beard, a hint of unkempt hair. He even wears his muddy boots into her house, indicating that he really doesn't think about things like decorum. He's showing that he's much more concerned about hard work and hiding himself than he is about presenting a clean image.

**Book Therapist Questions:** Who is your character? What sort of attire, behaviors, mannerisms and trappings go along with that identity?

Now, before you panic and think….wait, that's so stereotypical! I don't want you to write cardboard characters – don't panic! We're just setting up the components of the layers and, as you go, you'll discover even more facets to your character's identity.

2. **Noble cause/Purpose:** Behind every hero, there's a reason why he does the things he does. In *Braveheart*, the death of his bride compels William Wallace to fight for a free Scotland. In *The Bourne Identity*, it's Jason Bourne's quest to discover who he is.

In determining your character, you need to know what happened in his past that made him the person he is today. What was his darkest moment? Usually, it is this moment that contributes to his Noble Cause (and creates a superb foundation for letting the heroine see through his cracks to the vulnerable heart of the man inside).

Usually a person will do anything to make sure this dark moment is not repeated. Often the Noble Cause is directly related to either atoning for that dark moment, or protecting himself or others from it.

You'll use this information in developing a **Layer of Revelation.**

**Book Therapist Question:** What happened in your past that molded your goals and purposes today?

3. **Competence:** We like heroes who can take care of themselves, who know what they're doing. It builds our confidence in them and causes them to be heroic. What is that one thing that your hero does well?

*The Bourne Identity* is a wonderful movie that showcases Bourne's skills. We know that she is safe with him, even though many assassins are on their tail.

Even computer geeks can be heroic when we see them using their skills.

**Book Therapist Question:** What is your character good at, and how is that shown on the page? In a romance, you can go further and ask: What skills does your hero possess that he uses to save the heroine?

4. **Security:** When I'm plotting, I use the element of **Security** to pinpoint that point of no return, when a character must fish or cut bait. But when I'm working on layers, I use a character's *IN-security* to discover what his worst nightmare is. What are his deepest fears? What is he going to avoid at all cost?

Often you can discover these fears by going back to that darkest moment in the past. At some point in your story, your reader will be pushed to his limits. In that moment, he or she will either turn back to safety, or face their fears and move forward.

Discovering what he is most afraid of, what makes him feel most insecure, will add another layer to your character that will be revealed shortly before or after the dark moment.

In Donald Maas's workshops, he talks about finding that one behavior that your hero would never do. For example, building on *The Bourne Identity*, I doubt that Jason Bourne lets himself fall in love…and yet, there he is, falling in love with the heroine half-way through the movie.

**What prompts a hero to do something he would never do?**

**Answer:** His greatest fears pushing against him, his biggest dreams dangling before his eyes…and the realization that wants something different, something more. Bringing your character to this place, and revealing this for your reader, or heroine, is a pivotal emotional point on the journey.

**Book Therapist Question:** What is the one thing your character would never do, and what would make him do it?

5. **Belonging:** What lie keeps him away from God and why?
Because of your character's darkest moment, they will have learned from it, something that holds them back from happiness. We all operate with lies in our lives, and your character is on this journey to be set free. So, he must learn a truth, sometimes referred to as the Epiphany in order to maybe to be set free to compete his mission, or to be able to love. Understand this lie will help you create the last layer, the one closest to his heart.

**Book Therapist Question:** What lie has he believed that has broken him…?

Now, you should have interviewed your character enough to understand his Backstory, how he sees himself and why, what his motivations and goals are, what he has to live or fight for, what he's good at, what brought him to this place, what lies he believes, and what truth will set him free. These are the components you need to dress your character.

**Take your Character Deeper**

Okay, you're going to stop looking at other books and movies now…and turn your focus inward. I want you to interview your character. Yes. Sit down, have a cup of coffee in hand, lock your door, and imagine your hero (or heroine) in your mind. You are the therapist…and it's time to get to the bottom of things!

Basic Bio:
Name:
Age:
Profession:

Who are you? (Identity) How do you express this identity through your appearance?

What monumental event in your past shaped you and determined your goals and motivations for today? (Noble Cause/Purpose)

What are you good at? (Competence)

What is the one thing you would never do, and what would make you do it? (In-Security)

What is the lie that you believe, and what truth will set you free? (Belonging)

## Building the Five Layers of your Character

Okay, now we have the components to who he is…now let's clothe him in his layers.

**Layer One: His Attire:** (which reveals his Identity) mannerisms, clothing, public goals

Going back to the question about his identity, we're going to build an initial impression of our character, the one he gives off to our heroine, and our reader. There will probably be inaccuracies, just as real impressions are, but underneath the exterior, we want to glimpse his essential identity:

I'm going to read a few excerpts from a book I wrote a few years ago: *Escape to Morning.* The Hero is an undercover Homeland Security agent who is posing as a reporter. But Will's essential identity is protector. He is from South Dakota, so we'll dress him like a cowboy, and he's pretending to be a reporter, so he'll have some of those curious attributes as well. His goal is to get our heroine, Dannette, to trust him. Later on, she'll realize that he lied to her about his identity, but he can't totally divest himself of who he is, and we see this in the first layer:

Here's a scene where I reveal Will's first layer:

He *did* look sorry. She read it in his furrowed dark eyebrows, the grim slash of his mouth under his dark goatee, even the concern pulsing from his way-too brown eyes. The fury she felt dissipated from her muscles, leaving only relief. "I'm okay. And so is Missy."

He supported her arm as she rose.

Dannette had always been a tall person, able to look most men in the eye. But this near-killer stood a nose over her, and in his rumpled leather jacket, faded jeans and cowboy boots, he emanated a quiet, unobtrusive power. Maybe it was the way he held himself, feet planted his head slightly angled in concern. She felt his gaze run over her, and it wasn't at all invasive. "I didn't see her. It's a good think you yelled," he said it without defense, with sincerity.

Later she says:

Oh, a cop. No wonder he radiated this you're-okay-now-ma'am aura. Funny, with him standing a foot away from her, she sorta felt that way. Okay, now. All he needed was a badge and maybe a beat-up Stetson to complete his old-west-hero guise.

See how Will's identity as a protector shines through?

**Once we've established that first layer, we're ready to move on to our second layer.**

**Layer Two: His Behavior** (which reveals Character/Values/Competence): This layer reveals how he treats people, his habits (which also reveal values), his reactions to stress (which reveal past hurts and his essential character).

Our character's values and Noble Cause will begin to surface, even at the beginning, in small things, like when Will nearly kills my heroine's dog in the beginning, he takes her out for a meal. Yes, he's after information, but she's just come off a search and looked hungry and tired, and he wants to help her. It's that protector coming out in him.

This scene is from the hero's Point of View (POV)…and the first part is his protector instincts coming out…then it's a hint at his dark past, revealed through his habits and how he reacts to others.

Will rose and walked over to the far end of the room where, in a stone fireplace, a meager blaze sputtered, gasping for life. He took a poker, moved the ash-covered logs around, added another. He replaced the poker and grabbed a napkin from another table, and wiped his hands.

The woman said nothing, still cocooned in fatigue…or thought? as she twirled her fork.

"So, I never did get your name," Will said, returning to the table and squelching the urge to take the fork out of her hand. Tension laced the gesture and he felt the errant, and weird urge to help her unwind. He'd been on the dark end of body recovery a few times and knew that only time erased those images, if at all.

But, you also want the heroine to see it:

Obviously she hadn't totally run Cowpoke Masterson out of her head. And, if she were to be honest, he wasn't totally disgusting. Not with his devastatingly sweet smile. The way he helped her rub down Missy and settle her in the pickup had charmed his way too far into the soft spaces of her heart. She could hear the cowboy in his words, a soft western twang that spoke of broad skies, lazy days, slow laughter and sardonic humor.

In Will's POV, we dropped a breadcrumb about his past to reader, but we focused on his reaction to others in delivering that breadcrumb. Then, in Dannette's POV, we showed that he is essentially a gentleman. The idea is that we want to hint that there is more underneath that cowboy persona…through the eyes of both the characters.

And remember we're also trying to unlayer our character for the reader. *Often these two layers are revealed during Act 1 of the emotional journey.*

**Once his second layer is revealed through his habits and reactions to others, then you are ready for the third layer.**

**Layer Three: His Choices** (Which reveal purpose/Noble Cause): This layer reveals his external struggles regarding plot, his greatest dreams and why he thinks he'll never find them, his obstacles to love.

In every chapter, your character should have a conflict, or dilemma he has to solve. As you are facing those, you hint more and more at why his past and his Noble Cause determine those choices. You also want to reveal their greatest dreams. In this layer, you'll also reveal his competence, or the things he does well.

For example, after Will lies to Dannette (Dani), we don't want to hate him for his crimes, we need to hint at what his Noble Cause is that made him lie to her:

Will breathed deeply, suddenly missing the smell of prairie grass, the low of cattle as they roamed wide fields. How many times had he sprawled under the sky with Lew, hands behind his head, dreaming of their futures? Lew's always included Bonnie, and Will had endured painfully many torturous soliloquies of love and longing from his best friend.

Still, Lew had something that Will envied. *Still* envied. Honesty. A relationship with a woman that went beyond expectations. Bonnie had believed in Lew, had let him free to serve his country, knowing that Lew's heart stayed at home. Bonnie's love had given Lew a strength that Will still couldn't understand. Or maybe that strength came from something more.

Will put his hand to his chest, as if pushing away the burn inside. Memories of Lew always seemed to stir up the longings and attune Will to the vacancies in his life.

\*\*\*\*

See, now we know that there is something noble that Will wants – a home, a wife, a family…

Another technique to reveal this layer besides narrative is through dialogue – Letting the hero and heroine tell each other things about themselves – either deliberately or not – allows the other characters (and the reader) to know more about them. As their relationship deepens, it'll be harder and harder for him to hide behind his layers until he finally discards them, one by one.

Layer three is the longest layer to discard, so take your time, letting out information bit by bit. Have him share his greatest dreams with the heroine in one scene, and show your reader his Noble Cause through his actions. You may even want to have a conversation with a friend about the obstacles in his way to happiness.

**Eventually, your character will have to reveal Layer Four: His in-security:** His internal struggles, greatest dreams and fears, how he feels about love, his spiritual vacancies.

And this is revealed in two stages:

**Stage one:** His in-security is revealed through his *out-of-character* behavior.

In this phase of layering, you want to continue to put him into situations that confront his fears, force him to reveal his dreams to the heroine or to the reader, almost like turning the crank on a vice to make him open up.

One of my favorite scenes in *Escape to Morning* is when Will sees that Dani is headed for trouble – and again he has to choose between his mission and her safety. But he so desperately wants something between them, he can see that dream dangling right there before him…so he intercepts her, and blows his cover.

"Dani, it's okay," Will said, trying to keep his voice low, scanning his gaze past her, toward the cabin, past it into the dark fold of forest.

"What part of you scaring my skin off is okay?" Her voice shrilled, matching the white panic that hued her face. "And why do you have to always dress like a mercenary when you're in the woods? Good grief, Will, who do you think you're going to get in a fight with, a great horned owl?"

He couldn't hide the smile, nor it seemed his emotions. He'd seen her sneak up, and totally turned off the common sense screaming in his brain.

No, he'd been propelled by sheer panic.

But the fact that Little Miss SAR was back, and obviously fully charged, meant trouble.

And even more dangerous were the little feelings of happiness that were exploding all over his heart.

"Dani, please, for the last time, you need to leave."

"Give me one good reason." She held up one elegant finger. "One."

He made a face, opened his mouth. Okay, she had a point….without knowing it. He couldn't rightly explain without blowing his cover. But without blowing his cover, he couldn't get her to leave.

Besides, what if she were caught hiking out?

"Promise to listen to me? And, to obey me if I tell you to do something?"

She looked at him like he'd turned purple and spoken Russian.

"I know the words, 'You're not the boss of me,' sound slightly kindergartenish…but, *you're not the boss of me.*"

This time he really did stop her. Put all one-hundred-ninety pounds between her and her exit, and wore a face he hadn't used for quite some time. "You're not going anywhere without me, Dani," he said, slow and dangerously. "And I *am* the boss of you, starting right now."

Her eyes opened, and she backed away, tilted her head. "Now you're really freaking me out."

"Good. Please, take me very seriously. I know things you don't, and just suffice to say that they are part of my job. So, when I say things like, go home, which I realize you won't, trust that they are for your own good. Because I am your friend."

She swallowed, and suddenly he realized that no, he didn't want to be her friend. Not at all. In fact, he'd spent the entire morning lying when he told himself that it felt great to be trusted, that the feelings of honor she dredged up were enough.

He wanted more. Now that he'd gotten a taste of what it meant to be around her smile, her laughter, even her confused anger, he wanted more.

So now the hero is making decisions out of both sides of his brain: On one side, his *purpose* is propelling, the other side is driven by his dreams and/or greatest fears. And he's acting in a way he would never normally act.

**Stage Two:** His in-security is revealed through the *Sacrificial Act.*

Remember when we asked, *what would your character never do?* **This layer is revealed when he does it.**

This layer is Mr. Darcy's desperation, it's Hugh Grant in *Notting Hill* posing a question at the press conference. It's Jason Bourne saying goodbye to the woman he loves so he can be with her, later, whole.

Layers Three and Four usually encompass all of Act Two of the emotional journey. Take your time with them, don't bunch them into big revealing scenes, but drop them like tidbits to entice your reader on the journey.

For Will, he has to sacrifice his secrecy:

"Here's the bigger truth, Dani." His gaze burned into her until she turned. His eyes were dark, and she felt it on her, no, *inside* her. Touching her soul. "I know I'm not the guy you thought I was. But in every important way, I want to be. I want to be your friend, and...more. I want to be the guy that makes you feel safe, who you turn to when your dog is hurt, or you just need a hug. I want to be that guy who makes you home-made ice cream and buys you every dog movie on the planet." He swallowed. "I want to be God's man for you, today and every day. Please believe that about me."

Which brings us to the final layer, the layer in which we see our hero completely vulnerable... "naked" as it were.

**Layer Five: His Spiritual lie and the discovery of the truth.**

This layer happens when the Black Moment hits, when he realizes all his worst fears have come true. It's the beginning of Act Three in the Emotional Journey. You want to make him face the lie, and then be changed by the truth.

Here is Will's final layer: Dani is injured in the woods, but the clock is ticking on a terrorist attack, and he has the information to stop it, so he must leave her there, praying someone will come and rescue her, while he takes the information (and a girl named Amina) to safety:

> Just go.
> Those two words fueled every step, but pinged louder in Will's heart as he trudged away with Amina, feeling nearly nauseous. Fear pressed down on his chest and he struggled for breath.
> Just go.
> How could he leave her? He forced his breath through the web of pain and stared at the stars. The moon hung as a fingernail in the sky, pointing north. *Please, oh God, be our portion tonight.* Never did he long for those words to be true. Never did he need God more than this moment, when he'd left the best of all he wanted to be laying cocooned in his jacket under a black pine tree.

All of Will's layers are gone. He's figuratively naked, vulnerable. He's desperate, he's in love, he needs God…and we're rooting for him because he's completely captured our heart and we feel his pain.

As you build scenes, ask yourself, *What is the next layer I need to reveal for my character – to my other characters? To my reader?*

**But…what about prologues that reveal the dark moment of a character? Isn't that revealing a layer too soon?**

Yes!

I am a believer that prologues shouldn't be used unless they contribute to the mystery of the story. If the reader understands the character's darkest moment before they're ready, then it's cheating their emotional journey. The exceptions I would make are if a great deal of time passes, and if the emotional impact of the journey is beyond that moment.

A great example is a Deb Raney book (*In the Still of the Night*) that shows the brutal rape of a character at the beginning of the book. However, while this a dark moment, the real reveal is when they discover the identity of the rapist. This information is kept until the right reveal of that layer.

**Bring your character deeper:**

You've already built your character. Now, it's time to insert those layer-revealing moments into your story. Take your current work-in-progress (WIP). In what scenes will you apply the following layer reveals? (*My chapter suggestions are based on a 20 chapter book)

**Layer One: His Attire:** (which reveals his Identity) Mannerisms, clothing, public goals
(Hint: Commonly this is chapters 1-2)

**Layer Two: His Behavior** (which reveals Character/Values/Competence): Remember, this layer reveals how he treats people, his habits (which also reveal values), his reactions to stress (which reveal past hurts, and his essential character).
(This might overlap chapter 2, and continue through to chapter 4 or 5)

**Layer Three: His Choices** (which reveal purpose/Noble Cause): This layer reveals his external struggles regarding plot, his greatest dreams and why he thinks he'll never find them, his obstacles to love.
(You may show glimpses of this layer starting in chapters 3-4, and continue all the way to chapter 15)

**Layer Four: His in-security:** His internal struggles, greatest dreams and fears, how he feels about love, his spiritual vacancies.
(This might occur anywhere from chapter 12-18)

**Layer Five: His Spiritual Lie and the discovery of the truth.**
(Often this occurs near the climatic ending, anywhere from chapter 16-20)

## *Inserting Backstory*

But, you say, shouldn't the reader know more than the characters?

Yes. *Which is the Second Key to Deeper Characterization:* **Backstory Breadcrumbs**

*Oh Hansel, I'm so afraid no one will find us!*
*Never fear, Gretel, we will drop breadcrumbs, and someone will follow…*

## Creating Backstory Breadcrumbs

As you build your character and reveal his layers, you also need to keep in mind the balance between layering and dropping backstory elements that are essential to building the motivation of the character. See, your reader does need to know why your character is doing something. Not an entire diary entry, but just one sentence of information – and even that should only be the barest crumb of information.

The key to Backstory is dropping just enough crumbs to stir your reader's hunger for more. You don't want to give them too much at the beginning, or they'll get filled up, satisfied, and they won't have an appetite to finish the journey.

So, How much Backstory should you put into a scene? *Just enough to give the reader the information he/she needs to understand/accept the current action and decisions.*

They just need to embrace the character's motivations for continuing on in the journey.

For example, let's say that I have a character who has just inherited a ranch. I might open the scene where she is driving up to the abandoned ranch, looking at the life her uncle left her. Now, I might be tempted to go into a lengthy Backstory about how, when she was a child, she loved visiting the ranch, how she chased the prairie dogs and rode horses through the tall grasses, and how it gave her an escape from an alcoholic mother. I might go on to recall a conversation she had with her uncle, how he had one no-account son and she was like a daughter to him. I could even say that she'd spent the last five years as a lawyer in Minneapolis and was burned out after winning a child abuse case and wanted a fresh start because it reminded her too much of her own life. I could say all that. But it's *way* too much information for the beginning of a book, and really, it gives away the punch line. We want our readers to discover all this along the way.

Instead, I'll pare it down to the essentials:

"She couldn't believe that Uncle Henry had left her the ranch instead of Billy Bob. Nor could she believe she'd abandoned her law practice, especially now, after the victories of her last case. But maybe her uncle knew her better than she knew herself, had heard the silent pleadings of her heart. Even now, the wide expanse of the blue sky filled her soul like a spring breeze after a grueling winter, drawing her back to the land."

Okay, even that might be too much, but doesn't it raise a lot more questions for the reader? What silent pleadings? What case, and why would she leave? Who is Billy Bob? And what happened as a child to keep her tethered to the land? All these questions are Breadcrumbs to draw the reader further into the story.

In my book *Flee the Night*, the book opens with Lacey on a train, sitting next to her daughter. She sees a man get on – one she recognizes as an assassin. I drop only Breadcrumbs by pulling back on the information I give.

> The past couldn't have picked a worse time to find her.
>
> Trapped in seat 15A on an Amtrak Texas Eagle chugging through the Ozarks at 4:00 a.m. on a Sunday morning, Lacey . . . Galloway . . . Montgomery—what was her current last name?—tightened her leg lock around the computer bag at her feet.
>
> She dug her fingers through the cotton knit of her daughter's sweater as she watched the newest passenger to their compartment find his seat. Lanky, with olive skin and dark eyes framed in wire-rimmed glasses, it had to be Syrian assassin Ishmael Shavik, who sat down, fidgeted with his leather jacket, then impaled her with a dark glance.

In this opening scene, my heroine knows the man is he's after her, *but doesn't tell us why*. We also know she's protecting a briefcase, *but we don't know why*. And, we know that her past is bad, but again, *we don't know why*. All these problems are hinted at, but not solved. My goal is to lure the reader in with just enough Breadcrumbs to make them hungry.

**Book Therapist Question:** What is the *essential* information the reader needs to know to give sufficient motivation for the character? What story questions can you drop that will keep the reader interested?

Backstory Breadcrumbs are soft, tasty, *small* morsels to lure your reader into the story.

Using these two keys: Character Layering and Backstory Breadcrumbs, you'll find the right balance in deepening the connection your reader has with your character.

**Don't look back! Or…**

## The appropriate use of Flashbacks

One of my favorite parts of getting together with my family is reliving the Great Lund Canoe trip of 1981. My parents, always on the hunt for a great vacation spot for our family of five, decided that going on a canoe trip into the wilds of Quetico National forest in northern Minnesota with three unseasoned canoeists, one teenager who thought she knew more than she did, and the head of the household who had enough adventure in him for the entire family. We got lost, dumped all our purification tablets into a lake, nearly ran into a bear, accidentally trespassed onto private (Native American) land, and made it through by sheer grace from the fleet of angels who guarded us. The park ranger who gave us our permits said, when he picked us up ten days later, "Frankly, I never thought I'd see you again." We had similar thoughts (most of them voiced by my mother) during our harrowing adventure.

However, harrowing adventures make for great tales around the Christmas dinner table, and our family loves to talk about the day we got lost on a portage and ended up bushwaking through a swamp. Or the fresh blueberry pancakes (and narrow miss from the bear). Or the night we found the campsite in the pitch dark, at midnight (one of those providential moments). We laugh until we're crying, unable to speak.

And then we look up, at our guests and extended family members. They're staring at us like we might have just landed from the planet Zorgan, and are speaking Zorgonian. *Clearly, you have to have been there.*

This is when a Flashback, rather than Backstory, would come in handy.

## What is a Flashback in a Novel?

A Flashback is a section of novel that cuts back into time, and is told as if the character is actually back in that scene, experiencing events with the character. We see Flashbacks in movies like *The Fugitive*, when Dr. Kimble is remembering what happened the night of his wife's murder. Or in *The Notebook* (which is actually one giant flashback!) Or even television shows like Cold Case, or CSI. In the flashback, the view sees the event that happened, without the interpretation (but often through the eyes) of the POV character.

A Flashback is an essential part of Backstory that the author wants the reader to experience, in order to help them understand the real time plot or emotional journey of the character.

For example, in my book *Nothing But Trouble*, my character, PJ Sugar, has a pivotal black moment in her past with her former love Boone Buckam. Because that moment is so essential to PJ's Backstory and her emotional journey, it is key that the reader experience it.

Take a look:

She knew it was a dream, knew that she couldn't change a thing. Still, she tried—tried to change the wine-red dress she'd had tailor made, with the empire waist, v-neck, spaghetti straps, and shirred front. Tried to change the look on Boone's face when he picked her up, scrutinized her with those approving eyes.

PJ settled into the dream, feeling royal as she stepped from Boone's father's Cadillac, floating into prom on his tuxedoed arm. Roger Buckam stood near the door and nodded toward them. His eyes tight, he shook Boone's hand, his gold pinky ring glinting under the light of the torches that lined the walkway.

Couples strolled the golf course just outside the halo of light pushing through the club windows. Boone winked at her, then ushered her into the dance.

She hadn't been much of a drinker, even then, but when Trudi slipped her a taste of the liquid she'd poured into a medicine bottle in her purse, well, she hadn't been able to eat strawberries since without thinking of schnapps. She laughed too loud, even in her dream, danced hard, flirted well, and by midnight, Boone pulled her tight and offered an invitation that, even in her mood-heightened state, made her blush.

She'd agreed to meet him on the fourth tee, and he disappeared. *"Boone? Boone?"* She heard her voice, wondered if she spoke aloud, but then found herself at the pond, high heels swinging from her fingers. Overhead, the night sky played along with Boone's plans, stars winking at her, a slight breeze sullying a nearby willow, a golden near-full moon stealing her breath as well as any last remorse.

He loved her. Boone loved her.

And tonight, she'd love him back. A swirl of anticipation tightened inside her.

She heard laughter—Boone's, husky and deep, from the country club, and it lured her near enough to find him sitting on the back steps with his football cohort Trudi's date Greg Morris. Boone held the cigarette between his thumb and when he saw her standing barefoot in the shadows next to the dripping air conditioner. looked up at her like a deer in the headlights.

Yes, that's right, she'd heard him.

She vaguely heard him tell Greg to get lost as she yanked the cigarette from him. He found his feet. "PJ—"

"Don't even try, Boone." She stared at the cigarette, her entire body shaking. "You totally cheapened our . . . wrecked—"

A group of boys walked by—football buddies—and Boone lifted his hand in greeting. They laughed, and one gave him a thumbs up.

"What, does the entire school know?" She had the urge to fling the cigarette to the ground, but she was barefoot, and not about to put it out with her pedicure. "Here." She handed the smoke back to him. "That's the most 'fun' you're going to have tonight."

She turned away, sliding out of Boone's reach as he tried to catch her arm. Above her thundering heartbeat she barely heard the swish of her bare feet scuffing through the stubbly grass of the putting green. Even the trees seemed to want to hush her as she fought tears.

"PJ!"

He caught her on the tenth tee, his hand on her arm. She whipped out of his grasp, slipped on the slick grass and went down in a silky heap.

She felt ruined.

Boone knelt next to her. "I'm sorry."

He ran his thumb under her eyes, wiping her tears. "We weren't talking about you."

"Then who—"

But she never finished because he kissed her. Softly, his eyes in hers as he drew away. "I love you, PJ. I always will."

When he kissed her again, her arms went up, around his wide shoulders. Her breath mixed with his, and she could taste the champagne he'd snuck into the prom. She lost herself inside his embrace, moving into his advances, barely aware of her shoulders bared, how he'd managed to woo her nearly out of her dress, wrap her in his jacket, how he himself had lost his tailored shirt.

Her heart had already said yes, long before this night. It was only a matter of time before her body followed.

"Daniel Buckam, what in the—?"

Boone sprang away from her. PJ reached out to pull him back, but she'd already lost him as he found his feet, staring in horror at his father astride a golf cart. Sitting beside him sat Ben Murphy and, behind them, Ernie Hoffman.

PJ clutched Boone's jacket around herself, a hot embarrassment wrenching away her breath.

"Dad—"

"Don't, Boone. Get in," Buckam said coldly.

Without a word Boone obeyed his father, sliding onto the back shelf of the cart.

PJ huddled in the wet grass, unsure what to do.

Then Director Buckam gave her a look that made her want to curl into the fetal position. "What are you waiting for?" he snapped.

Murphy crooked a finger at her. But Ernie smiled kindly, patted the seat beside him.

PJ turned her back to them, pulled her dress closed, shivering, shaking. Feeling naked even as she zippered herself back together.

And Boone didn't look at her.

She tried to find defense—wasn't prom night the perfect night? And it wasn't like it was a first for the country club, or even, probably, this green. Still as she climbed on beside Ernie and they raced back to the clubhouse, she felt like a tramp.

And then she got it.

Smoke spiraled off one end of the country club. Near the restaurant. Where she'd taken the cigarette from Boone.

Thick and black, the smoke chewed up the night sky, devouring their prom.

She glanced at Boone. He'd gone pale.

Buckam stopped the cart and got out, and PJ expected him to address Boone. Instead he grabbed PJ by the arm and hauled her over to the chief of police, who gave her a look that cleared the final passion-fog from her brain.

"Here's our little arsonist," Buckam said as smoke teared her eyes.

She looked over her shoulder and caught Boone's eyes. *What?* But Boone was the one with the cigarette—

He turned away, his hands in his pockets.

The smoke could still make her tear, fill her lungs with acrid pitch. She coughed.

Coughed again, her chest closing upon itself. Coughed again, so violently it woke her.

She sat up in bed, still feeling the bruise of her cough.

Smoke.

A thin veneer crept into the room in the early morning light, but because of her vast experience she recognized it in a second. And, as if in confirmation, the fire alarm went off, numbing nearly all thoughts save one.

"Davy!"

I could have written it as pure Backstory narrative:

PJ's prom night had been a fiasco. Not only had she discovered her boyfriend saying lewd things about her to his football buddies, but later, as she'd sank into his arms on the tenth tee of the country club, they'd been discovered by his father. Worse, she was later blamed for burning down the country club.

Although that is all accurate information, it doesn't deliver the impact we need to understand the significance of the event. This one event causes PJ to leave town and not return for ten years. It also builds the tension between PJ and Boone when she does return because Boone let her take the blame for the fire (although she was innocent). Finally, it's a key element in PJ's emotional journey because she discovers truths about this even that alter how she sees herself.

In this case, creating a Flashback is the only way to deliver the impact of the event.

However, here is a scene that shows us a piece of PJ's Backstory, in narrative form.

PJ had just turned eight the first time she left home. She remembered the crisp air redolent with decaying loam, pumpkins with saggy eyes peering out from doorsteps, and cornstalks hung from front porches, tied with baling twine. Auburn leaves crunched under her feet, and a slight northern wind bullied the cowboy hat she'd pulled over her jacket hood as she hustled down the road, kicking stones before her with red galoshes. She balanced a stick over her shoulder, and a handkerchief tied to the end held a soggy peanut butter and grape jelly sandwich and a few stolen peanut butter cookies. Enough to get her through the night, during which a wagon train headed west would find her and collect her for their journey to Oregon and the Little House on the Prairie. And should they happen to run into any renegade outlaws, she knew just how to handle them—with her six gun cap shooter tied to her leg.

PJ traced her first escape route as she drove toward her mother's home, remembering how big the hill had seemed, how cold and ominous the pond, dotted with shiny oak leaves. She'd reached the railroad tracks crossing Chapel Hills when her father pulled up in his '85 Jaguar, a sleek green lizard, rolled down the window, and stuck his elbow out. He looked regal with his thick black hair, those rich green eyes, a grey worsted wool suit against a black tie. "It's gonna get cold, PJ," he said. "And your mother has stew on."

PJ still made a face, even in her memories.

He had laughed. "All good cowgirls eat stew."

PJ remembered the way she crawled into the car, sliding on the sleek leather seats, smelling his cologne. He wouldn't be home long—probably had a meeting to attend, somewhere—yet for that moment, he'd been her champion.

She still missed him most in the fall. "Your cowgirl finally left town, Daddy."

Why didn't I create a Flashback for this? Because although it gave resonance to PJ's feelings about her father and her innate wanderlust, it isn't necessary to build the current plot, or even PJ's emotional journey. It's simply a piece of Backstory.

**How do we decide when to use a Flashback or just insert Backstory?**

A Flashback should only be used when the scene or event that happened in the past is both *complex* in nature – meaning, it has many facets to it that relate to the character's emotional journey – as well and *relevant* to the storytime plot or emotional journey of the character.

Let's create a two-part Flashback litmus test to help us understand when to use a Flashback, and when to use Backstory.

**It is Complex?**

A Backstory layer is usually rather simple – one event that influenced the character and moved them forward, or taught them a lesson. It can usually be explained with one or two sentences, and the reader legitimately understands the impact of the event.

A Flashback, however is a significant event that so influenced or changed the character that it affects the storytime's current plot, and the character's emotional journey. Because of this, a Flashback has many facets.

For example, in PJ's Flashback, we understand Boone's significance, we understand her feelings about the country club, fire, the teachers who found her, and we are there, feeling her shame as the entire town watches her get arrested. There are so many facets to this horrible event that affect her life, she'd have a difficult time summing it up.

And we use this difficulty the **Complexity Litmus Test** to determine when to use Backstory or Flashback. We simply ask our character: Describe the pivotal event in your past.

*Scene 1:* PJ says: I was kissing my boyfriend on the golf course, in my prom dress, and well, we'd been going out for a long time, so I thought this would be the night, but he wrecked it by telling all his buddies, but of course, I forgave him anyway, and while we were in the middle of…you know, his father of all people drove up and found us, along with two other teachers from the school – one who happens to be the dead guy I'm trying to solve the murder of – and while they were unhappy to see Boone and I in a love pretzel, they were really after me, because they'd heard that I'd set fire to the country club because I'd been smoking…which I hadn't been…and that's another long story…
Okay, I think you know the answer to that one.

*Scene 2:* PJ says: When I was ten, I tried to run away from home. I didn't get very far before my father found me, pulled up in his fancy car, and persuaded me to go home. He understood my wandering heart better than anyone else.

Easy.

See, Scene One, the country club fire is complicated and affects the plot of the story on many levels. Scene Two is simply added character texturing.

So, the Complexity Litmus Test confirms the need for a Flashback to reveal all the facets of the event.

### Is it Relevant to the Storytime Plot?

The Flashback must bring something forward from the event that is integral to the storytime plot. It could be a motivation, a plot element, a character lie…something that matters in the current plot. I also must have an emotional element to it that requires the character to think about it, or confront it during the journey of the story. Thus, to be a Flashback, it must past the **Relevance Litmus test.**

Again, let's examine the two scenes. In the first scene, we meet a number of people who matter to the current plotline – Boone, of course, and his father. But also Ernie, who is found deceased a few days into the story. Also, since PJ is still harboring hurt over the event, and since Boone is still trying to get into her good graces, their past contributes to their current conflict. Finally, PJ's issues of shame still affect her today, and her emotional dark moment in the book relates directly back to that event on prom night.

In the second scene, between PJ and her father, the moment where PJ is remembering her father passes as soon as she drives up to her house. Yes, it's a sweet memory, but there is no intrigue about the event and since her father is deceased, he brings no conflict to the present. It's not a moment that needs to be relived, or even remembered, if we were tight on word count. Thus, scene one passes the Relevance Litmus Test.

Now that we know if we should use a Flashback or simply Backstory, let's establish some **Flashback Rules** on how to use a Flashback.

**Rule #1. Thou shalt not use more than three Flashbacks in a book**. And, if possible, thou shalt keep them to ONE major flashback per book.

Why? Because if you have too many flashbacks, it dilutes the story, and it gets confusing. The reader needs to focus on one pivotal event that shapes the plot or emotional journey today. If the event is too large, and you need to break it up into two or even three events, then insert them in pieces throughout the story. You may also have two events that lead up to the third, major event. Or three examples of the same kind of event.

For example, in the Fugitive, we see three major flashbacks of the story – the first is when Dr. Kimble is describing to the police what happened. The second is when the trial takes place and we see Dr. Kimble's wife calling for help, and thus why he is convicted. The third is when he chases down the one arm man in his home. All three of these are portions of the same scene, but they work together to reveal more information each time. The few snippets he has of being with his wife are backstory elements, not true flashbacks.

The exception to this rule would be if you are writing a dual story, where there is a dual plot, one in the past, one in the present. Rachel Hauck's *The Sweet By and By* is a dual plot story and concise but vivid flashbacks make up a subplot within the main plot. Books like The Time Traveler's wife and the Outlander are actually stories with two plotlines.

**Rule #2. Thou shalt use clean construction to move the reader in and out of a Flashback.**

First, let's start with the understanding that we will *not* making the flashback in different typestyle. I know the temptation is to set it apart from the regular story. I have done that in situations where the flashback is, for example, actually a piece of correspondence, or even a dream, but it can be very jarring for the reader.

Instead, here are a couple techniques for entering and exciting a flashback seamlessly:
Going into the flashback, you first want to alert your reader to the fact that it is not happening in the storytime present. Give the reader some hint that you are travelling through the mind of the character to a different time.

> He remembered the moment like it might be yesterday.
> Her words brought him right back to that moment when...
> He stared at her, but saw through her, into the past, right when.....
> He blinked, and then he landed right there, in the past...
> Or, as in the excerpt above, which is a dream/flashback – She knew it was a dream,
knew that she couldn't change a thing. PJ settled into it... etc.

> Once you're in the flashback, you use one or two "hads", putting the scene into a past perfect grammatical construction, making sure your reader is soundly into the flashback, and then continue on simple past.

> She hadn't been much of a drinker, even then, but when Trudi slipped her a taste of the liquid she'd poured into a medicine bottle in her purse, well, she hadn't been able to eat strawberries since without thinking of schnapps. She laughed too loud, even in her dream, danced hard, flirted well, and by midnight, Boone pulled her tight and offered an invitation that, even in her mood-heightened state, made her blush.

> She'd agreed to meet him on the fourth tee, and he disappeared. *"Boone? Boone?"* She heard her voice, wondered if she spoke aloud, but then found herself at the pond, high heels swinging from her fingers.

The scene continues on in simple past tense until we reach the end: The smoke could still make her tear, fill her lungs with acrid pitch. She coughed.
The use of could brings out of the past with the conditional past. I could have also used the past perfect construction – "The smoke had made her tear, then, and it tasted as real now as it filled her lungs with acrid pitch. She coughed."

Then, bring your reader out of the flashback, and settle them firmly back into the present, with the standard simple past construction.

> She sat up in bed, still feeling the bruise of her cough.
> Smoke.

A thin veneer crept into the room in the early morning light, but because of her vast experience she recognized it in a second. And, as if in confirmation, the fire alarm went off, numbing nearly all thoughts save one.

Note, too that I give some nod to the fact that she had been in a flashback: still feeling the bruise of her cough. It's a way to make us realize that the scene we just witnessed was real, although in the past.

The use of proper technique when entering the flashback, melding it seamlessly into the prose, will allow your reader to move in and out of it without feeling jarred.

**Rule #3 Thou shalt not have another Flashback, or excessive Backstory within a Flashback.**

Oh, you know what I mean. You're in a flashback, and suddenly you remember something that your reader needs to know – so you just go ahead and stick it into that flashback. Wrong. You are confusing your reader.

I know. I did it. Here's a passage from *Tying the Knot* – my second published book (so cut me some slack) where I insert Backstory into a Flashback. In this scene, my hero, Noah, is remembering the initiation into the gang, and how his life started to derail. Just a note: today, this scene would NOT pass my Flashback Litmus Test, but I was a young writer back then…

What an idiot he'd been – over a bag of tortillas chips.
Shorty Mac had shoved a 9mm Glock into his hand as they crouched in the shadows. Cold and heavy the weapon send a thrill of fear though him as they watch the Tom Thumb convenience store, waiting for L'il Lee's sister to emerge. "She's unlocking the back door," Shorty Mac said, a devious glint in his eye.
Noah hadn't seen the deceit even then.
Shorty Mac, childhood friend turned homeboy had learned well in a month's time how to lie with the best. But Noah had believed him and inched toward the back door. The October wind whistling under his Chicago Bulls jacket. He counted it a triumph when he'd five finger discounted it from a local mall, despite the fact that he'd yet to wear it home. Mother Peters would have skinned him alive if she suspected gang colors in her foster home. Noah's heart panged thinking of the Native American woman who'd given him over a decade of 110% mothering complete with anguished prayer and tough love.

This section highlighted is backstory. Now, in my defense, I cut it way back from what it was – a mini-scene of him actually stealing the coat! But we don't need to know where he got the coat, or even about Mother Peters, who we meet later. It slows the flashback and confuses the reader.

Flashbacks should be a clean scene, free of commentary by the pov character. The reader should simply see it as a frame of reference to understand later.

**Rule #4:  Thou shalt show a Flashback, not tell it.**

A Flashback is a mini scene – with the five senses and dialogue and action – it's not unlike time-travel where the reader is allowed to "flash back" with the character to relive their past. Because of the very nature of a Flashback, it is easy to show instead of tell. However, just to be clear, narrative summary does not a Flashback make.

What do I mean?

Here's an example of narrative summary trying to masquerade as a Flashback:

PJ had felt royal as she stepped from Boone's father's Cadillac, floating into prom on his tuxedoed arm. Roger Buckam shown his displeasure in his eyes, even though Boone had ignored them, ushering her into the dance. Music played and all her friends had been there, greeting her. But she only thought of Boone and what she'd promised him that night. How was she to know that her promises would turn to ash?

She had something to drink. And later on, she stumbled out to the back of the country club where he was with his friends. She heard them saying some nasty things about her, but told herself that Boone loved her. Over and over she said it, even though she would regret it later.

Which is why she went out and met him on the tenth tee. And that was where his father found them an hour later.

That is pure narration. Yes, it happens in the past, but there is no dialogue, no real time action, no emotional layering into the story. We are not present in the scene with PJ, we're simply remembering it through her telling of it. She is layering in her interpretation of the event, not letting us relive it with her.

Now, here's the scene (again) in flashback form:

PJ settled into the dream, feeling royal as she stepped from Boone's father's Cadillac, floating into prom on his tuxedoed arm. Roger Buckam stood near the door and nodded toward them. His eyes tight, he shook Boone's hand, his gold pinky ring glinting under the light of the torches that lined the walkway.

Couples strolled the golf course just outside the halo of light pushing through the club windows. Boone winked at her, then ushered her into the dance.

She hadn't been much of a drinker, even then, but when Trudi slipped her a taste of the liquid she'd poured into a medicine bottle in her purse, well, she hadn't been able to eat strawberries since without thinking of schnapps. She laughed too loud, even in her dream, danced hard, flirted well, and by midnight, Boone pulled her tight and offered an invitation that, even in her mood-heightened state, made her blush.

She'd agreed to meet him on the fourth tee, and he disappeared. *"Boone? Boone?"* She heard her voice, wondered if she spoke aloud, but then found herself at the pond, high heels swinging from her fingers. Overhead, the night sky played along with Boone's plans, stars winking at her, a slight breeze sullying a nearby willow, a golden near-full moon stealing her breath as well as any last remorse.

He loved her. Boone loved her.

And tonight, she'd love him back. A swirl of anticipation tightened inside her.

We are just moving into the Flashback here, but already we are outside with her, hearing her voice as she hunts for Boone. We are experiencing the scene – and later the disappointment – with her.

Move back in time in the skin of your character, don't just let her tell the reader what happened. Show…don't tell.

### Finally, **Rule #5 Thou shalt not create entire chapters of Flashbacks**

Keep the flashback fairly short. You want it long enough to build the scene, showing the who, what, where, when, and why of the scene, and employing all the scene elements, from the five senses to dialogue to active verbs and nouns. However, if it is longer than three pages, then the reader maybe pulled too far in and unable to remember what is happening in the present time. You're just giving them a glimpse of the past, not trying to resettle them there. Get into the Flashback, get to the point of the Flashback, and get out.

Otherwise, you may leave your reader behind.

Flashbacks can be a very effective way of building plot, or creating emotional conflict for your character's journey, if they pass the Flashback Litmus Test of Complexity and Relevance.

And if you remember the Five Rules for Flashbacks, you won't get lost in the wilds of storytelling, and you'll be able to keep your reader paddling ahead.

**Bring your Character Deeper:**

Number your chapters and your scenes. (I'll help by creating a chart!) Now…what does your hero have to accomplish in the scene, and what is the least amount of information your reader needs to know to embrace or understand his actions?

| Chapter/Scene | Goal for the scene | Backstory Breadcrumb |
|---|---|---|
|  |  |  |
|  |  |  |
|  |  |  |
|  |  |  |
|  |  |  |
|  |  |  |
|  |  |  |
|  |  |  |
|  |  |  |
|  |  |  |
|  |  |  |
|  |  |  |
|  |  |  |
|  |  |  |
|  |  |  |
|  |  |  |
|  |  |  |
|  |  |  |
|  |  |  |

| | | |
|---|---|---|
| | | |
| | | |
| | | |
| | | |
| | | |
| | | |
| | | |
| | | |
| | | |
| | | |
| | | |
| | | |
| | | |
| | | |
| | | |
| | | |
| | | |
| | | |

Now that you understand the Character's Emotional Journey, how to layer and unlayer your character and drop Backstory Breadcrumbs for deeper emotion, let's get to the specifics.

## Writing Character Emotions

I do a lot of traveling. Not long ago, I was sitting in O'Hare Airport when a woman walked into the gate area. She was in her early twenties and carried a backpack, which she held with a whitened fist. She sat down and began to fidget in her seat, checking her watch, looking at the gate, pawing through her bag. She pulled out a book and clutched it to her chest a moment before opening it, and pulling out a highlighter.

The book's title said, in large black ominous letters – *How to Get Over Your Fear of Flying*.

Periodically, she wiped her hands on her jeans and blew out a long breath, as if she'd been holding it.

I decided I would call her Darla.

About five minutes before we began to board, Darla called home. I know because she spoke into her cell phone loud enough to be heard all the way over in Detroit. "Dad, I'm getting on the flight now. I'll see you soon. Yeah, I'm so nervous, I can barely breathe, but I'll be okay."

I could almost hear the pleading voice behind her words saying, "I hope I hope!"

I said a little prayer for her and got on the plane. I had a window seat.

Of course Darla appeared not ten minutes later, checking out the row numbers, and stopped at my row.

Darla had the aisle seat.

She unpacked her backpack, shoving her *How to Get Over Your Fear of Flying* book and the highlighter into her seat pocket for easy access, and then shoved her backpack under the seat. She buckled her seatbelt, pulling it down tight. She gripped the armrests and did what I considered early-labor breathing. A sweat dribbled down her brow.

She was starting to freak me out.

Then she looked over at me, opened one eye and said, "I'm a little nervous."

You think?

The short version of the story is that I ended up holding her hand during the takeoff of the flight. More importantly, watching her made me realize that she was a classic example of the four layers of character emotions.

*A reader doesn't want to be told what to think and feel.* They want to discover the story along with the characters – embrace the lessons, experience the pain, and rejoice with the victories. The best stories are the ones that invite the reader into the emotional life of the characters, and make a reader invest so much that they can't put the story down.

*But how does an author write emotions that draw the reader in and allows them to experience the story?*

As we begin to apply the character's emotional journey to the page, slowing unlayering them, we need to understand the four layers of writing emotions and when to use each layer. We also need to understand the colors of emotions – meaning the different hues that go into big emotions and how to enhance one hue for greatest emotional impact. Finally, we'll work on a step by step approach to building the right emotion so as to connect with your reader in a way that resonates, and touches the heart and soul.

## The Four Layers of Writing Emotions

The first layer of writing emotions is simply that surface emotion **– The name of the emotion.** Darla turned me and said: *I'm a little nervous.* She stated her emotion.

*If I were to write this, it might look like:*

> She stood at the entrance to the gateway and her heart filled with fear.
> She could not watch the children on the playground without feeling sorrow.
> Never had she known such happiness as when she saw her son walk off the airplane.

Naming the emotion is a common technique – probably the most common and easy to write. Most people can connect with these feelings and generally can relate to the character. But does it prompt a visceral response? Probably *not*. The author is just accessing that information level of the brain. The reader is agreeing with that emotion, but not necessarily feeling it.

We use this technique a lot for quick emotions, for emotions that are part of creating the emotional components of the scene. We might also use them as an introductory statement to a paragraph about that emotion or another. Finally, characters might use this technique when they are describing other characters (e.g., Fear flickered across her face.)

Naming the emotion is a tool to set a tone or for general description of a scene or character. It is the not the main emotion of the scene. It does not work to draw our readers into the heart of your character.

*So, let's go to the next layer:*

Poor Darla said, "I'm so nervous I can barely breathe." Yeah, that made everyone in the gate area feel better. But through that admission, she connected a little more deeply with us.

This layer is called: **Just Under the Skin Layer. This layer names the emotion and pairs it with a physical response.**

> Fear clogged her throat.
> Dread prickled her skin.
> Her heart twisted with sorrow.

We, as readers understand what it might mean for fear to clog our throats. We understand dread prickling our skin. Putting a physical response to the name of the emotion helps a reader apply their own physical response to the situation. Yes, I've been so afraid that I can barely speak, so I understand the visceral feeling of fear the author is trying to convey. The author is now connecting the reader to the character on an informational and physical level.

This technique is used for those deeper emotional moments, something significant that the author wants to use to draw the reader deeper into the emotional experience of the character. It's used to accentuate the actions around the emotion.

> Fear clogged her throat as she watched the policemen step onto the doorstep.
> The door locks clicked. Dread prickled her skin.
> She watched the woman gather her son into her arms, and her heart twisted with sorrow.

This technique is useful for helping the reader understand the state of mind of the character, putting them in a place of sympathy with the character. The reader can relate, even remember when they have been in a similar place, but it doesn't cause their own physical response.

*Let's go deeper:*

Sweat dribbled down her brow. Darla gripped the seats with whitened hands. She practiced early labor breathing.

Even if I hadn't heard her on the phone, just by her actions I would have understood what was happening. I don't need to know the emotion to know she was afraid.

**The next layer is simply the physical response only. I call it the Touching the Heart Layer.** It's where the reader says, "I have *so* been there." The reader sees the behavior, or physical action, and the physicality of it reminds them of when they were in the character's exact place.

Here's some phrases an author might use that are simply physical:

> Her pulse ratcheted to high. (fear)
> Her breath caught. (surprise)
> She swallowed hard, her throat parched. (dread)
> Her skin prickled at his touch. (creeped out)
> Fire streaked through her, right to her toes. (desire)

The reader is deeper into the character's skin because they aren't told what emotion to equate with the sense, but rather are left to experience the sense and apply their own experience and emotions to it. We, as the reader, have to dig around our hearts to decide what emotions that might be, and when we find it, we understand on that heart-level what the character is going through. You *know* I felt sorry for that woman when she began her pre-labor breathing.

This is where a lot of authors stop. They have connected with their readers hearts, made them feel what their characters feel, and that's their goal.

But there is another layer, one that goes even deeper, one that makes us connect with the character, an almost spiritual, definitely life-changing connection.

**And that layer is called Soul-Deep.** It's the use of Action, Metaphor, and other Characters to convey emotions. *It's the heart of showing.*

Let's look at Darla again: Darla had a book. The *How to Get over Your Fear of Flying* book. She takes it out. Clutches it herself, and then almost frantically shoves it back into the bag. Then, after wiping her hands on her pants, breathing out a few times, staring out the window, she grabs it again, and this time opens it, tearing off the highlighter top with her teeth and going to town, marking up the book, as if it holds the key to surviving the next two hours. The book is hope and promise and victory and I saw in my author's mind's eye a two-year-old clutching his blanket, trembling and alone in the middle of the night in his crib.

Don't you feel sorry for her?

Gary Smalley calls the technique of communication creating a "word picture" – and suggests that married couples use it as they communicate soul-deep feelings. When people can connect to a word picture, they can connect to the emotions we are trying to covey. For authors, if they can connect to a word picture, then they can connect to that emotion and all the different hues of that emotion. Darla's teddy bear book communicates fear, and desperation, and the need for salvation, as well as the promise that she could overcome her fear of flying. We, the reader, understand all those hues, and instead of being locked inside one emotion, we're allowed to feel the entire array.

It's this connection to your character that will glue your reader to the page. If I were to write this scene in Darla's POV, using this metaphor, it might look like this:

> She didn't need the book. Didn't need…okay, maybe she'd just take it out and hold it. She didn't want it get lost, maybe left behind. She pressed it to her chest, stared out the window at the airplanes, like birds – safer than cars, the book said – moving around the shiny tarmac. Clear blue skies. A perfect day for flying.
> She put the book back in the bag. Shoved it deep. Zipped up the bag. Really, it wasn't like it was a security blanket, or that she was a toddler. Across from her, a woman with an iPod looked away – Darla knew she'd been staring.
> She blew out a breath. Rubbed her greasy palms on her pants. Maybe she should call her father – again. A voice came over the loudspeaker. She tried to listen, but lost the first half of the announcement. What if it if was her flight, what if she was left –
> She unzipped the pack and wrestled out the book. Opened it. There – "Preboarding, what to expect at the gate."
> Had she read that chapter? She pulled out the highlighter, held the cap in her mouth and began to underline. Probably she'd just keep the book out.

In that scene, I never mention that she's afraid. But the reader sees it in her greasy palms, and breathing (there's the touch the heart layer) but most of all, the reader gets into her skin through the symbolism and action of needing the book like a security blanket. See, we, the reader, don't just feel her pain in our hearts, we've been there, wanting to defeat something, and not able to. We've now connected with her on a spiritual level, one of deep understanding, because we understand the metaphor.

And we understand the defeat when the fear wins.

**Bring your Character Deeper**

Take a break and walk over to your bookshelf. Open a story that has touched you, and take out your highlighter. (Four highlighters of different colors would be best!) Now, open the book and see if you can identify the four layers of the story, and when they're used.

Go ahead and take some notes:

Examples of **Naming the Emotion**:

Examples of emotional layering **Just Under the Skin**:

Writing that **Touches the Heart**:

Setting, Action and Metaphor that reveals the layering that is **Soul-Deep**:

## Building the Soul-Deep Layer into a scene

First, I want to start out with a challenge I deliver to all my Book Therapy clients: Write the scene without naming the Main Emotion of your character.

What? Yes – if you can convey the emotion without naming it, and draw your reader deep into the skin of your character through the use of a metaphor, then you have written a story that will linger with your reader. You've allowed them to experience the story with your character.

So, if I can't name that emotion, how do I work it into a scene? You put emotion in a scene through the use of **Setting, Characterization** and **Action.**

### 1. Setting

Consider this little passage from my book *Finding Stefanie*

Gideon turned off the highway and headed west. He glanced at the gas gauge, gripped the wheel of the old Impala wagon he'd boosted, and scanned the darkening land for shelter. He supposed they could sleep in the car, but the way the wind had kicked up, throwing frozen tumbleweeds across the road, he'd prefer shelter. And a fire. And something nourishing in their stomachs.

At least for Haley. . . . He glanced in the rearview mirror at the way she curled into a tiny grubby ball inside a red Goodwill winter jacket two sizes too large for her. One of her pigtails had fallen out, lending her a forlorn, lopsided look. And her eyes screamed hunger. But she didn't speak. Hadn't spoken one word since they left the shelter.

The tires moaned against the highway pavement, like the sound of a siren in their wake.

How do you feel about their situation? Desperate? Fearful? The reader doesn't know it yet, but Gideon has kidnapped his two sisters from a child shelter. I never say he is desperate or on the run, but I convey it in the description. Wind kicking up, throwing tumbleweeds, a grubby Goodwill jacket, pigtails falling out. Eyes screaming hunger.

And then I interject a little metaphor, using sound to convey his fear that someone might be following him.

Here's another excerpt from later in the scene:

He passed miles of barbed wire fencing and dirt driveways that led to tiny box homes with feeble light showing from the windows. He guessed the black humps against the darkening horizon had to be cows or maybe bulls. Here and there the tattered outline of trees edged a hill, boulders lumping in washes.

He would have missed the house entirely if it hadn't been for Macey, who spotted the *For Sale* sign tangled in the barbed wire fence. She saw it flash against the headlights and said simply, "Hey."

Do you feel his sense of aloneness, that he's driving deeper into his desperation? Feeble light, black humps, tattered, edged….all these words give a sense of uneasiness to the scene. And then, I insert the For Sale sign, tangled in the fence, showing the house unwanted, uncared for. The perfect place for Gideon and his sisters who feel the same way.

Why do we get scared when a character walks down a creepy basement? We don't even need to know that she's afraid (in fact, sometimes we're more afraid than she is). It's the setting that makes us afraid.

**Book Therapist Trick:**
1. Pick verbs that convey the emotion you're trying to establish. Kicking, screaming, throwing – all can convey as sense of panic, or doom, or fear.

2. Use specific and revealing nouns when describing a scene. Specific nouns carry emotion. Tumbleweeds, a Goodwill jacket, barbed wire.

3. Find one metaphor that you can interject into the scene that captures both the feeling of the scene and the emotion you want to convey.

*Here's what I do* – I write the scene. Then I go through and change the verbs to match the mood. I delete any verbs that aren't focused and any nouns that aren't conveying the emotions in the scene. Then, I look around and find one metaphor from the scene that I can apply to evoke the emotion of the scene.

Let's take Darla on the plane. How do we convey how she feels about entering the airplane? We might use the stuffy, conditioned air and turn it into a metaphor of noxious gas poisoning her as she walks on to the plane. Or, the seat belt pinning her to the seat. Maybe we could see a metaphor in the rows and rows of fellow victims, all surrendering their lives into the hands of an unseen protector, not unlike worshippers kneeling before an altar. Then the door closes, forever enclosing them inside, like a tomb.

I don't know about you, but with those kinds of verbs, nouns and metaphors, I want to run down the aisle screaming, and make them open the door!

Use your setting and description to convey emotions through verbs, nouns and metaphors.

## 2. Characterization:

Use other characters to build emotion into a scene. Sometimes, we can project the emotion of a character onto another character, almost like a mirror. Other times, we can juxtapose it. This is called **Character Comparison**.

This is from a scene later in *Finding Stefanie*, when she happens upon Macey, Gideon's sister. Stefanie is feeling out of place in her own life….

His sister leaned against the truck, arms folded, face dirty. She had black hair—so black that Stefanie knew it had to come from a bottle—and a number of piercings up her ears and one over her eye. Whatever makeup she'd once worn, it had trailed down her face, or maybe that was simply soot. She wore a black shirt under her jacket and a pair of black jeans that looked like she'd painted them on.

Stefanie had had a pair of jeans that fit like that once. Caused her more trouble than she wanted to remember.

Stefanie takes a look at Macey, and a part of her really understands her. Macey **mirrors** her messy, even angry, emotions. Not only that, but Stefanie feels compassion for her, which will play into why, later, she offers Gideon and his sisters a home.

Let's go back to Darla and show her emotions through a juxtaposed **Character Comparison**.

Across from her, a woman's sandaled foot tapped to unheard music, her eyes closed, her hand draped over her carry-on bag. In her other hand she held an empty coffee cup from Starbucks, as if she'd started her morning early. Sure, fatigue pressed into the wrinkles of her dress pants, flattened her blonde hair. However, she hadn't a hint of sweat, nor even a crease on her forehead as the gate attendant announced their flight. Indeed, in moments she'd bounded into line, handing over her ticket, wearing an expression that suggested she'd finish her nap in-flight. A regular Amelia Earhart.

Darla sees a calm, if not tired, passenger. Hopefully you can hear some envy from Darla, some wistfulness that she might be that calm, even accustomed to flying.

Character Comparison is just a matter of letting your character see someone who embodies the same or opposite emotion as your character, and letting them describe them in their voice, adding inflection, opinion, and using strong verbs and nouns to convey that emotion.

**Book Therapist Trick: Look around the scene**. Who do you have in the scene who might have been there, done that, in terms of your character's emotions. What do they look like now? Or is there someone your character would like to emulate? Or even, is there someone your character would never want to be?

Now, describe them, again using those emotion-packed verbs and specific nouns, and throw in a metaphor.

3. **Action**

Action is one of the strongest ways to creating that emotional soul-deep connection.

I love the movie *P.S. I Love You*. There is a wonderful scene right after her husband's funeral where the heroine is alone at home with her grief. We know she's sad, but when she climbs in bed and calls his cell phone and listens to his voice mail message over and over, and over, it's heart-wrenching. She says nothing, but it's powerful.

This is a scene from *Taming Rafe*, book two in the Noble Legacy. It takes place right after he's discovered that Kitty – a girl he's come to love – is engaged to someone else.

Rafe slammed his way upstairs, banged open his bedroom door. The entire house shook. Crossing the room, he ripped his Bobby Russell and Lane Frost posters off the wall and grabbed the box of videotapes he'd dug out for Kitty. He took his trophies, his ribbons, his two championship buckles, and the scrapbook he'd kept for himself over the years and shoved them into his PBR duffel bag. Then he threw them all over his shoulder and stormed back downstairs.

He took the back roads to the burial mound, driving as fast as he could without dropping one of the axles. He stopped at the bottom of the hill, lugged out the bag, and muscled himself up the hill.

He threw sticks and twigs together, and taking a lighter he'd found in Piper's glove compartment, he knelt and lit a blaze.

The flame crackled as it devoured the sticks, then the kindling, and finally the larger pieces of wood he added for fuel. The flame showed no distinction between the fragile and the hearty, biting into the wood with tongues of orange, red, and yellow.

Rafe opened the duffel. Instead of dumping the entire thing on the flames, he pulled the items out one by one. His posters. They burned in a second, curling into tight balls. The ribbons, which sent out an acrid odor. The scrapbook. The fire started on the edges, burning away the accomplishments, the defeats. Then the tapes. The smell of plastic burning made his eyes water and sent black smoke into the now bruised sky. The trophies would take hours to fully burn, but their plastic mounts deformed and caved in on themselves immediately. Finally, the buckles. He dropped both of them into the flames.

The flames crackled, spitting and popping as they devoured his life. The bull rider. The man Kitty claimed she believed in.

Then Rafe drew up his good knee, crossed his arms atop it, buried his head in them, and for the first time since his mother died—even during Manuel's funeral, even in the dark months that followed—Rafe let himself cry.

I only have one physical action – Rafe let himself cry. But you feel his erratic emotions as his truck careens over the hills, and the despair as he tosses his life into the flames. I also throw in a metaphor – the fire making no distinction between fragile and hardy – meaning that heartache can happen to anyone. I hope you can feel his pain.

**Book Therapist Trick:** When you're exploring the action of your emotionally packed scenes, ask what is the *one* thing your character could do to convey the *main* emotion of the scene. Then, accentuate that and build your metaphor into that action.

**Bring Your Characters Deeper**

Take a scene of deep emotion in your current WIP and make it Soul-Deep.

**Step one:** Find the one emotion you want to convey.


**Step two:** What nouns, verbs and metaphors can you build into the scene to convey the emotion of your character?


**Step three:** Is there another person in the scene you can use for character comparison?


**Step four:** What is the one action you can do to convey the character's emotional state?


**Now, write the scene without naming the emotion!**

## The Colors of Emotion

Using Setting, Characterization and Action to convey emotion is only the first step. As the author, you need to go deeper. A great book doesn't explore just the typical responses to say, grief or love, but goes deeper and explores the **Shades of Emotions.**

We all know the different phases of grief: Shock, Denial, Bargaining, Guilt, Anger, Depression, Acceptance. There are a plethora of books and movies about this process. Why, because grief expresses itself in an array of emotional colors.

*All emotions have colors to them.*

Love has desire, hope, security, fear of change or loss, possessiveness, jealousy, generosity, patience and kindness.

How about Anger? Guilt, frustration, panic, loss, jealousy, power, helplessness. Even anger has an array of emotions.

Because any given emotion can feel unwieldy and large, picking a hue allows the author – and the reader – to focus on that one aspect and connect that particular hue, exploring the different aspects of that emotion for a deeper experience.

What about Darla's emotions? She's afraid. But in that fear is also hope for redemption. And jealousy that others aren't afraid. She's probably also panicky. And needy.

So, as an author writing her scene, I will draw out one those hues and accentuate it. Let's use panic. And let's illuminate it through action. I'm also going to throw in some characterization, and lots of strong verbs, nouns and metaphor…

> Darla strapped herself into the seat, shoving her book into the pocket – not too deep. Outside the baggage handlers threw the suitcases like hot potatoes onto the ramp, as if sensing a countdown.
> She sat back. Adjusted her belt. Pressed her fingers to the book. Across the aisle, the three seatmates were chatting, as if over coffee. The woman next to her had fallen asleep, and the passenger next to the window, oh, great -- Amelia Earhart bobbed her head to her music.

The flight attendant's voice boomed over the speaker. Darla fumbled through the pocket for the instruction card, then glanced over at her seatmates. They hadn't moved. She yanked the card from the adjoining seat, and slapped it onto the lap of the irresponsible woman next to her. Then she poked the be-bopper and gestured to the front.

She'd missed the first part about the oxygen masks. Wait! And how did they put them on – *wait!* She raised her hand, but the flight attendant didn't stop. She waved it even as the woman moved onto a discussion about floatation devices. What floatation devices? She scraped her finger down the card, where –

A flight attended bumped down the aisle. Darla dropped the card onto the floor and lunged for her arm. She wrapped her whitened fingers around it in a death grip. "Remember the flight in California, where the oxygen masks didn't drop?"

Every eye had turned to her. Even the be-bopper had pulled her buds from her ears.

And just then, the engines fired up. The sound tore through Darla like a scream, tearing through the passenger cabin and right into her bones. *Where was that oxygen mask?*

The flight attendant pried her fingers from her arm, and twisted free. "I promise, we're going to live through this."

Yeah, sure they were.

The Anger hue I used was *Panic*, but note that I never mentioned the emotion. Instead, I used a metaphor of the hot potatoes to suggest the sense of panic from the baggage handlers. I also juxtaposed the casual demeanor of the other passengers, talking as if over coffee in Character Comparison, and I used a sound for the big emotional metaphor – the engines screaming – which is what Darla wants to do. But mostly I convey the action of panic through Darla's actions, and finally her death grip on the attendant.

And note my use of verbs and nouns: Instead of tucking her book in the pocket, she *shoves* it in the pocket, instead of pulling the card out of the pocket, she *yanks* it, then *slaps* it down on the lap of her seatmate. She *pokes* the other woman. She *lunges* for the flight attendant. Even, the use of the tongue in cheek term, *Be-bopper* tells us that she's annoyed that the seatmate isn't paying attention. All these words contribute to building a scene that conveys her panic. These are color words and they illuminate her emotions.

Although I wanted to convey fear, it's a big emotion to handle. Instead, I picked a hue to really focus on, and it strengthens the entire emotional impact. And, don't worry about hitting the right color words on the first pass - that's what rewriting and editing are all about.

*A great book doesn't tell a reader how to feel. It draws the reader into the scene, step by step, through information, physical responses, and metaphor, focusing on the right emotional hues and using color words to help immerse them reader into the vivid scene, so that they to can be red hot angry, or bluer than blue.*

**Book Therapy Trick:** Find the *main* emotion your character is experiencing, then break it down into its different hues. Pick one of those hues to focus on, using metaphor to connect your reader to that emotion.

*Note:* I was talking with a client recently about MRU – Motivation Reaction Units. We were talking about what *order* to put the emotion into the scene. Here's my advice: *Be the character.* If you are in his skin, what happens to you first – do you hear the information, or do you react to it? It'll depend on the situation and the information relayed. The point is, if you want your reader to react with you, then you, the author, need to think beyond telling them how to feel, and bring them on the journey with your character.

### Bring your Character Deeper

✓ Using the scene you just worked on, can you find the hue to accentuate in the scene?

✓ Rewrite the scene, focusing just on that hue. Does it make the scene even tighter? The emotion crisper?

## Encouragement from your Therapist

Phew. Tired? I'm sure you are. Writing is hard work, and tapping into the emotional journey of your character is exhausting. Often, we have to tap into our own memories or reserves to adequately bring the right emotion to the page.

I'll bet you're thinking…wait, really? Do I have to do all this? Can't I just write the character by the seat of my pants? Why do I have to plot it all out and add all those layers? Yes, the information about the emotional layering is helpful, but really, I see books all the time that don't go that deep and they're just fine.

Yes you do. They're *just fine*. But, are we stopping at *just fine?* Or are we trying to connect with the reader in a way that stirs their heart, even their soul?

First – if you are not a plotting person, don't worry. Most writers are a combination of plotters and pantsters. I myself like to plot the structure and journey of the story, then discover the scenes as I write them. I start out with scene goals and let the characters lose from there. But having a grid, or a flow for your character's emotional journey, may help as a idea-starter, or even as a checklist after you've written the book to make sure you've included all the elements.

Also, if you're wondering where to take your character next emotionally, trying looking at his layers – is he ready to reveal another facet of himself?

Finally, when you write your scenes, just lay them out on the page. Then take them deeper, according to the type of scene and what you hope to accomplish. At least now you have some ideas and tools on how you might do this.

Writing a book is exhausting. And rewarding. And when you get a letter from a reader who says she laughed and cried and pondered her relationships with others, and God, then I promise, it'll be worth it.

Don't just be fine. Be *the Finest*.


Let's press on and learn how to make our plots Wider!

# Section Two: Wide Plot

A book with great characters will still fall flat with a predictable plot. We, as readers, want something that makes us look up from a book with our mouth open, our hearts racing as we wonder just how it could get any worse. Or why we didn't see *that* coming? Or even shaking our heads at the amazing twist in the story. A great plot is a balance between the predictable and the unbelievable, one that makes the reader say, "Wow! What a story!"

But how do you develop those plot elements that leave the reader's jaw dropping? How do you sprinkle into it those pieces that suddenly fit together at the end? How do you think "outside the box" with plot without going so far out that your reader says, "Oh, that couldn't happen" and throws the book against the wall?

If you've read *From the Inside-Out*, then you learned how to develop a basic plot based on your characters wants, fears and dreams. Now, building on that, it's time for some plotting pieces that will bring your plot wider, reaching out to include Subplots and layers. In the WIDE section, you'll learn how to insert those pieces early on that will fall in place in final stages of your story. We'll talk about the big picture plot, how to create scenes that make your hero heroic, and how to ramp up the plot tension by reaching beyond the obvious, without drawing in the infeasible. You'll discover how to keep that tension high with the balance of stakes versus motivation. You'll learn the difference between a Subplot and a story layer, and when to use both, as well as the place of secondary characters in a story.

And then we'll brainstorm scenes you might insert into your plot to widen it.

Then, as a bonus, we'll talk Villains – how to create the perfect Villain, and their role in plotting your story.

Taking your story WIDE is about adding those secrets and techniques to your plot to make it something that leaves your readers not only surprised, but glued to the page until the wee hours of the night.

Let's get started.

## Why and Why Not?

Why is William Wallace (*Braveheart*) the perfect candidate to fight the war for Scotland's freedom? Because he's lost his wife, and he understands better than anyone what is at stake.

Why not? Because his grief could blind him and make him trust the wrong people. And, let's not forget England is far superior in size and strength over Scotland.

Why is Dr. Richard Kimble (*The Fugitive*) the perfect hero to discover his wife's murderer? Because if he doesn't, he'll be executed for a crime he didn't commit.

Why not? Because he's on the run from the police, and there is an investigator on his tail who is as savvy as he is. And that investigator doesn't care about Dr. Kimble's innocence.

Why is Frodo the perfect Hobbit to take the ring to Mt. Doom? Because he isn't tempted to let the ring control him like the humans, elves and dwarfs are.

Why not? Because he's a little Hobbit, unaccustomed to adventure.

**Why and Why Not?** They are questions that should be posed at the beginning of every character's journey. Romance writers use it for developing the connection between their hero and their heroine. But any good plotter uses it to develop their character's journey. Without a Why Not, it's too easy for your hero to succeed on their journey. Without a Why, there is no motivation for them to try.

The answers to Why and Why Not can't be something frivolous or easy to dismiss. They must connect to the core of who the character is, some event they've experienced, or belief they have that propels them forward. The Why should be something so compelling they can't turn away from it. The Why Not should feel insurmountable.

Let's look as some other popular movies:

Why is Luke the only one who can stop Darth Vader? Because he is his offspring and the "Force is strong in him!" (Because only Luke can free his father).

Why Not? Because Darth Vader is his father, and the pull towards the Dark Side also flows strong in Luke!

Why is Jason Bourne the only one who can figure out his identity? Because only he has the desire to unlock his past – the agency wants him dead.

Why Not? The further he gets into digging into his past, the more it repels him.

Why is John McClane the only one who can save the hostages in *Die Hard 1*? Because no one else knows that he is there, or that they are hostages, and his wife is in the middle of it.

Why Not? Because he's the only one standing between them and their well-thought out plot, and there are a team of assassins after him.

It's seems easy, but the truth is, discovering the Why and Why Not early on in your story is essential to building the plot devices you'll use later.

**How to discover the right Why.**

**The Why must have two components:**
> *Core (or value-based) motivation*
> *Uniqueness*

**Core Motivation:** The Why of the character's journey must be motivated by something so powerful that it pushes them forward despite the Why Nots before them.

Think about the elements that push us forward – usually the elements that motivate us the most have to do with our core values, the things that mean the most to us.

This spring, I had double-booked two events – a writer's conference, and my daughter and son's prom party. I throw the prom party every year, and since my son was a senior, I knew I couldn't miss it. Likewise, I was honored to be able to teach at the writer's event, so I couldn't cancel. Instead, I asked that all the classes fall at the beginning of the conference. Then, I got up at 4 a.m., drove two hours to the airport, got on a flight, caught yet another, landed, and drove another three hours to arrive one hour before my kids left for prom. The journey felt a little like *Planes, Trains and Automobiles*, but I was propelled by my value of wanting to celebrate the triumphant moments with my children. More than that, I wanted them to know that I was committed to their important events, despite my schedule.

Let's go back to *Braveheart* – the Why of his journey starts when he marries his wife in secret so that he might not have to share her with the lords of the land. Freedom is at his core, and when she's killed, he knows that he must fight for a free Scotland. It's not just about his wife's death – it's the cost of slavery to their English masters.

Dr. Richard Kimble's journey begins the night his wife is brutally murdered. He can't believe they are accusing him of murdering her when he, at his core, is a man who saves lives. In fact, he is busy saving a life while she is getting murdered, and later we understand that he was the intended target. Had he not been saving a patient's life, then he would have been there to protect his wife. Protecting his wife – even after the fact – is at the core of his journey.

**So how do you find your character's core motivation – that plot element that will drive him through the story?**

It's a matter (of course) of going back to your character interview and discovering that thing that matters most to them. **Often you can start by taking a look at their identity** – who they are.

Dr. Richard Kimble is a doctor, therefore saving lives is paramount to him. When he can't save his wife's life, he is driven by his value of protector to find her killer.

William Wallace is a warrior – if you remember the story at all, his father and brother were brutally murdered when they were ambushed by the English in his youth. When he returns to his village as a grown man, it isn't as a warrior. Still, he opposes the rule of the English, and their right to take the brides of the Scotsmen on their wedding night, and thus, convinces his bride to marry in secret. When she is menaced by soldiers, he finds himself fighting for her – until she is killed. Suddenly he's an outcast and a troublemaker…a warrior. And at the core of his fight is the value of freedom.

Frodo is a Hobbit, and the Hobbits love the Shire. When Gandalf gives Frodo the ring to flee with, telling him the Shire is in danger, Frodo flees. It is his love for home and the threat against is that causes him to step forth and become a Hero-Hobbit. Behind that is his value of family and home.

*Ask your character:*
Who are you? What is your identity and why?

Then, when they define for you their identity, look for the core values inside it. Freedom? Loyalty? Patriotism? Family? *This core value is what will drive them forward in the story and give you the first component of Why.*

**The second component of Why you need is Uniqueness.**

Only your character can accomplish this journey. Whether it is because of their unique past, or abilities, or determination, or beliefs, or even physicality (e.g. being a Hobbit), their uniqueness is the other half of the Why.

Only Frodo can carry the ring because Frodo, as a hobbit, has a pure and simple heart and is not swayed (much!) by the ring's power. Unfortunately, this is not true when we discover that Gollum was a Hobbit. But as they begin this quest, it is clear that only Frodo can carry the ring. Add to that that Frodo comes from the lineage of Ring Bearers – his uncle was the first to have discovered the Ring. Both of these unique traits combine to strengthen Frodo's Why.

Only Dr. Richard Kimble can solve his wife's murder. Only he believes/knows that he is innocent, and only he has the memories that can unlock the mystery.

Only William Wallace has the leadership elements needed to lead the rebellion against England. His father was one of the original leaders who was murdered by the English, so William has grown up with a legacy of loss that has fueled his passion for freedom. And, most of all, William has nothing to lose.

How do you find that unique element that creates the other component of Why? Go back to that interview you did with your character as you were building their journey, and look at their competence. What are they good at? Why? What unique skills, abilities, personalities, physical attributes, legacies, even knowledge do they possess that sets them apart?

Luke wasn't just a Jedi. He was the son of Darth Vader.
John McClane wasn't just a New York cop. He was the wife of one of the executives.
Jason Bourne wasn't just a guy who lost his memory. He was a trained assassin.

*Figure out your character's competence and you will discover their uniqueness.*

Before you can incorporate the Why in your story, you need to discover the Why Nots.

**Why Not?**

What stands in the way of your character accomplishing their mission? The Why Not needs to be something that is equal in menace and strength to the character's Why. It needs to be so big that if it weren't for the power of the Why, the character would turn back, giving up on their quest.

How do you discover the Why Not?

Here are some ideas:

*The Great Why Not can be found by looking at your character's goals, and then turning it over to find the opposite goal.*

William Wallace wants to lead Scotland in a rebellion. His goal is a free Scotland. The opposite would be to disgrace his country and he leads Scotland into defeat. How might that happen? What if he turns out to be a bad leader, or even reckless enough to lose the respect of his people? What if they turn against him? Why would that happen? If his desire to win made him vulnerable to bad judgment, then that would make a compelling Why Not.

John McClane's goal is to stop the takeover of the Takayama Tower and save his wife. The opposite would be for the thieves to get away with the goods, and to kill his wife. How might that happen? By cutting off communication, and making sure he is outmanned and out-armed. The Why Nots require John to go it alone against a team of well-armed assassins.

Luke's goal is to fight Darth Vader, and bring him over to the right side. Thus, the opposite would be not only if Luke can't bring Darth over to his side, but if Luke is also sucked over to the Dark Side, instead. How might that happen?

See how the plot is built around thwarting the main goals of the character?

**Book Therapist Question:**

✓ What is your character's goal?

✓ What is directly opposite to that goal?

✓ How might that scenario happen?

*Now here's the key to making your plot WIDER: Once you figure out the great Why Not, give us a glimpse or taste of it in the beginning of the book.*

We need to believe the Why Not is possible, that the character might **fail.**

Within 24 hours of Dr. Kimble's train wreck/escape, he is nearly captured, and must leap off a giant waterfall to escape. Worse, the detective after him announces that he doesn't care if Dr. Kimble is innocent. His only job is to capture him. The viewer is clearly aware of the Why Not, and that Dr. Kimble could fail.

William Wallace marries his woman in secrecy, thinking he can live in "freedom." But when English soldiers menace her, he can't stand by, and kills them. He escapes, but she is captured and murdered. His desire to be free has muted his fear of English brutality.

Frodo's goal is to get the ring to safety, without it possessing him like it might another creature. However he succumbs to his curiosity and puts on the ring, which allows the Ringwraiths to wound him on Weathertop. Frodo is not invincible.

Following the Why Not, gradually show us the **Why.** Plot two or three key scenes that reveal your character's **Core Value** and **Uniqueness.**

Scenes like:
      Wallace dreaming about his woman, and having her wake him for battle.
      Dr. Kimble saving the life of a child, despite the personal stakes to himself.
      Frodo hiding under a tree and staying calm as the Ringwraiths breathe over him.
      Jason Bourne driving the car through the Paris streets after one look at the map.
      Jason washing Marie's hair.

Establishing the Why and Why Not will also allow you to boil down the essential elements of the plot and help you craft your premise. It's the first step in making your plot WIDER.

**Make Your Plot Wider**

Let's add some scenes to establish the Why/Why Not for our character!
*Brainstorm:*

    A Failure/Why Not Scene

    A Why Scene revealing his Core value

    A Why Scene revealing his Uniqueness

## Acts of Heroism

Now that you've figured out the Why and Why Not of your story, along with the big plot obstacles, it's time to widen your plot with: **Acts of Heroism**.

**Acts of Heroism** are those character-change actions that take your character from an everyday Joe to a Hero.

It's not the grand gestures, the great sacrifices…Acts of Heroism are the everyday acts of our character that push him beyond himself. Ideally in a story, every choice your character makes and every step beyond his comfort zone that he or she takes, is going to push your character farther and farther from the person he starts as, until finally he becomes a full- fledged hero.

Let's go back to two of my favorite movies - *Eagle Eye* and *Cellular*

*Eagle Eye* is the story of an everyday guy faced with the accusation that he's a terrorist. He has to figure out how to stay alive – with someone else controlling his life, and of course, prove his innocence. It's a breathtaking movie. Jerry Shaw is not very heroic at the beginning. He's actually kind of a shyster, which we see when he cons his friend out of cash at a poker game. However, he turns into a full-out hero by the end of the book. Actually being willing to sacrifice his life for his country.

In *Cellular*, another thriller, an everyday young man with issues of laziness and irresponsibility is pulled into a kidnapping/hostage situation when he receives a random call on his cell phone from a woman being held captive. Step by step he's pulled into danger, as he tries to rescue this woman, each choice causing him to be more heroic until finally he puts his life on the line to save someone he doesn't even know.

How do these two everyday Joes turn into heroes?

Acts of Heroism.

And not just any heroic acts, but the type that move your character from **Primal Instincts** to **Noble Sacrifice**

### What are Primal Instincts?

Power, love, survival – These are the basic instincts, the primal instincts, of nearly everyone.

Less primal are things like revenge, greed, and comfort.

Most characters begin their journeys fueled by primal instincts. We all act out of a basic emotion – however, some are more noble than the next. As your hero moves along the spectrum, he'll have opportunities to choose increasingly more noble options, and each option will make him more heroic.

For example, Consider Jerry Shaw in *Eagle Eye*. The first heroic thing he does is to stay with the woman instead of leaving her in Chicago, even though he wants to. He doesn't do it for her son, but rather his own survival. Then, his next choice, he has to rob a bank. He doesn't want to – but this time, he does it to save the woman. And, after that, his subsequent choices are made to save the woman's son – and ultimately his country. As his primal instinct choices become more noble, his heroism becomes more clear.

As your hero proceeds on his journey, make each choice he makes more noble, and he will become more heroic until finally he must make a Noble Sacrifice to save the day.

And who doesn't love a character who makes a Noble Sacrifice?

As you plot your story, make sure that each Heroic act is more noble than the last, and your plot will become wider.

**Book Therapist question:**

Where does your hero begin his journey?

What is the Noble Sacrifice he makes at the end?

## *Stakes versus Motivations*

Or, driving your reader through the story through the use of Rising Stakes and Motivations.

Why should a reader pick up your book? Why should they care about your story?

**Stakes.**

The Stakes are the key to any winning story – the higher the stakes, the more epic a story. Another way to look at it is…what will happen if the hero fails his quest? Mordor will take over Middle Earth. The Empire will prevail. The aliens will take over the planet.

But not all stories can have world destruction at the core of their plot. Maybe the story is simply about finding or losing your true love. *The Princess Bride. Sleepless in Seattle. While You Were Sleeping.*

The key isn't how big the stakes are, but how deeply they hit home with the reader. The more personal the stakes, the more they resonate at our core, the more we will not only believe them, but embrace them. Stakes can be used as motivation to drive a reader through the story, and turned into obstacles to give your reader and your character "something to fight for."

Stakes can be public (affecting society, like in *Raiders of the Lost Ark, The Hunt for Red October*, or even *Erin Brockovich*), or private (as in some of my favorites: *Frequency, Cellular*, or even the poignant *Somersby*). The important element is: If the stakes matter to you, they'll matter to your readers.

**Public Stakes**

Public stakes have much to do with public values. For example, during World War Two (WWII), the public value was very much protecting our country and banding together to fight the wars. So, stories about espionage and battle were popular stakes in books and movies.

However, as time has changed, so have our values.

Today, personal freedom and family have taken over as the chief collective stakes of today. We still have issues of national security (which is why shows like *24* are so popular). But even within those issues, it is shows like *Army Wives*, which focus on the personal life behind the war that captures people. When stakes involve our freedoms and safety as Americans, or members of a family, it makes for a compelling story.

One example is *Saving Private Ryan*. Even the main character – Tom Hanks – realizes the power of family within the great backdrop of the war as he fights to bring home Private Ryan to his devastated mother.

A story stake that had, for example, saving the shoppers in a mall from a terrorist's bomb, or keeping a disease from becoming an epidemic and sweeping across the nation would be a current public stake.

*Ask*: What matters to me? If it matters to you, then it matters to others. What's the worst thing you could think of happening to you? Others will fear that also. And that's where you find your Public Stakes.

But what if your story is more personal? What if it only affects a family – perhaps it's the story of a child that is kidnapped, or one of my favorite episodes of *Little House on the Prairie*: Laura and the Horse race.

Who can forget the story of Laura Ingalls, where she rides her horse Bunny in a race against Nellie? Evil Nellie hates that Laura has a horse, and persuades her mother to buy her a fancy horse from Mankato. Laura's horse doesn't have a chance in the race against this thoroughbred. What's worse, Mrs. Olsen mocks Caroline for being poor and refuses to sell her shoes for her children until she has cash. If Laura can win the race, she'll receive a prize that she can use to pay for the shoes. She trains Bunny and is ready for the big race when Willie (Nellie's brother) gets sick. No one is around, so Laura has to make a choice: Ride Bunny to fetch the doctor and risk the horse being too tired to run the race, or let Willie suffer. What will she do?

We care about the outcome of this story because it has tapped into our values of family honor and compassion.

These are **Private Stakes.**

Private stakes can be found in the root of our values. The things that drive us, or the things we long for. Laura longed to show up Nellie, and to help her parents. But she also knew that to be true to who she was, she had to be compassionate. When we tap into our private stakes, it touches the core of our characters, and our readers, and gives them as reason to fight. You know I was sitting on the edge of the sofa, (or more likely standing up, cheering) as Laura ran the race with Bunny.

How do you find those personal values of your character? Here are some simple **Book Therapist questions.**

✓ What matters most to him in life?

✓ What would he avoid at all costs, and why?

✓ What are his goals, and why?

As you interview your character and plot your story, see if you can discover the Stakes of the story.

You will use both Public Stakes and Private Stakes as fodder to create obstacles and motivations for your character as you plot your storyline.

Discovering the Public and Private Stakes are only the first step in creating a compelling story. They must then be used to create story stakes and motivation and then put to the right rhythm and balance into the plot to create a riveting sequence of events. A great story requires a careful balance of rising story stakes and strengthening motivations not unlike the rhythm of the one–two punch. They work together to create a can't-put-it-down novel.

But how do you pick the right story stakes, use them for maximum effect to create a knockout best-seller?

105

## Let the Fight Begin!

One of my favorite movies for continually raising stakes and forcing the viewer to the edge of her seat is the thriller, *Cellular*. Just to recap, in a nutshell, it's a movie about a woman who is kidnapped. She uses a demolished phone to call for help and gets hold of a young man whose girlfriend has broken up with him because of his irresponsibility. A deadline of sorts hangs over their conversation (an essential element in any suspense), because, at any moment, they could get cut off, and she may never be able to dial out again. She must convince this random guy to help her. He eventually gets involved to the point where he begins to break the law and risk his life to save her.

Why does he do all this for someone he doesn't know? It's certainly not to prove he's responsible. He actually doesn't agree with the accusation by his girlfriend. So what makes this free-living guy care enough about a stranger to help her?

The answer is found in the rising balance of story stakes and motivation.

We learned about the different kind of kind of stakes: public and private. Now as you lay out the stakes, you're going to make them fit your story.

First, you'll make sure they are in **Proportion** to the challenges before the hero. If the stakes are too great, the hero will simply give up.

For example, by the end of *Cellular*, the hero is taking on bad cops in the LA police department who are trying to kill him. If he knew at the beginning of the movie what he'd be facing in the end, he would have hung up the phone in an instant. But in the beginning of *Cellular*, only the life of the woman is at risk – and frankly our hero doesn't even believe her. All that is at stake for him is that he'll be late running an errand for a friend. (Thus cementing the idea he's irresponsible). The stakes are miniscule, and he doesn't need much private motivation to overcome them.

He takes his cell phone to the police station rather dubiously, and is told he has to take the phone to the next floor. He's losing reception on the phone when he hears her being attacked. Suddenly, the stakes are raised. The woman's life *really could* be in danger. Suddenly we're beginning to tap into his values (responsibility). He isn't going to let the phone go dead. Now what? The author raises the stakes to a new level. The woman's son is threatened. The hero makes a heroic choice (one step above his primal instincts) when he decides he must race to the school to find the boy…only to have school let out a sea of khaki and blue shirt clad ten-year-old boys. He is too late to reach the child, and watches him get kidnapped.

New Stake: The child has been kidnapped by thugs. It is met with the new Motivation: A child's life is in danger, and the hero didn't reach him in time, thus he feels responsible. Our hero makes yet another heroic choice when he races after the bad guys, all the while dodging traffic.

Then the cell phone battery begins to die. It's yet another stake in the story, compounded by the fact that he's lost the bad guys. In that moment, our hero makes a pivotal choice to hold up a cell phone store for a battery charger, crossing the line to a point of no return.

Why?

Because the stakes have been raised. His belief that now two lives are at stake, and that only he can help (Why!), trumps the challenges before him. If he'd, say, grabbed the plate number, and called it into the police, or believed that the victim might call someone else for help, he might not have had sufficient motivation or belief in the stakes to confront the challenges before him.

Now that the motivation – that only he can help – have been raised to meet the stakes – the two lives on the line – the author raises the stakes yet again, threatening the husband. And after our hero has conquered the challenge of saving the husband…the author raises them again with a final stake – good against evil.

The key element here is the harder a character has to fight to win the day, and the more he has to fight for, the stronger the reader will stay hooked to the story. But each rising stake in the story must be in proportion to the motivation the character has to overcome it.

The second element to weaving stakes into your story is to create **Believability.** If, say, our hero was suddenly being chased down the street by a tank, in the middle of LA, well, we might react the same we did to crazy movies like *Volcano*. But even in *Independence Day*, we believed each outrageous stake because they'd gradually brought in the aliens and destroyed the cities in a way that seemed plausible.

Every increasing stake in *Cellular* is believable, or explained easily away, from losing reception (he is in an old building with cement walls), to why he can't rescue the child (the kids are all in uniform, and the school lets out just as he arrives, into a flood of blue-shirted tykes). As you create your stakes, make sure there is one simple, believable explanation for that rising stake.

The final key in keeping your plot riveting is **Balance.** The stakes must rise in rhythm to the motivations. If you raise two or three stakes at once, then you need to ensure the motivations are strong enough to overcome it.

For example, in *Cellular*, if our hero's cell phone battery was dying, someone was shooting at him, and he got into a car accident and broke his arm all at once without stopping to insert rising motivations, he might throw in the towel. His motivation just wouldn't be great enough to face those cascading stakes. However, if the bad guys got a glimpse of him, and promised to go after someone he loved, he might find the strength to dig himself out of the rubble.

Make sure that you're balancing those stakes with motivations in a rhythm that keeps your hero moving forward instead of crushing him. And remember – the higher the stakes and the faster they pile up, the more tense the story. So, it behooves the author to save those techniques until the end of your story.

**You'll notice too, that each time a stake is raised, another element of his Primal Instincts is brought into play.**

*Proportion, Believability* and *Balance* are the keys to propelling your character through a story, over obstacles and challenges and even to the point of your hero risking it all for a stranger and becoming an ultimate hero.

**Book Therapist Question:**

✓ For every challenge or turn in the story – have your raised the stakes sufficiently?

✓ Are the characters current motivations high enough to face those stakes?

**Make Your Plot Wider:**

I have a rule of thumb: Every 50 pages, I raise the stakes. That's about every 10,000-12,000 words. Or every three or four chapters. Using the plotting chart, and starting with the inciting incident, chart the rhythm of stakes and motivation in your story. Don't forget to make your hero more heroic with each decision!

| Chapter | Stakes | Motivation to overcome Act of Heroism |
|---------|--------|---------------------------------------|
|         |        |                                       |
|         |        |                                       |
|         |        |                                       |
|         |        |                                       |
|         |        |                                       |
|         |        |                                       |

## *Peripheral Plotting*

What if the book feels too linear, despite the rising stakes and motivations? Or perhaps it feels only about power or survival? How do you make your character pick through his Primal Instincts to find the more noble one?

*You need to employ some* **Peripheral Plotting!**

Peripheral Plotting is the technique of pulling in ancillary elements and using them to create more tension in your plot. Ideally, they will make your character have to tap into a more noble instinct and push them along their journey.

### How does Peripheral Plotting work?

I'm going to veer away from *Cellular* and *Eagle Eye* for a moment – only because they are such straightforward plots, and look at *Live Free or Die Hard* the latest in the Bruce Willis saves the world saga. *Live Free or Die Hard* is a perfect example of peripheral plotting.

Basically, through the Internet, the bad guys are trying to take over all the transportation, finances and utilities in the United States, and if they succeed, the entire world as we know it will collapse. Fascinating, big stakes, and the Primal Instinct here is survival. The problem is, that after a while, we as the viewer become bored or hardened to these larger stakes, and the Primal Instinct to save the world – and survival gets old.

Ultimately, we only care about stories that touch our hearts, and frankly, survival of the world, while important, just feels untouchable. Thankfully, the creator chooses to make it personal, to require John McClane to become more noble by making the situation personal. He kidnaps John's estranged daughter and threatens her life.

*Suddenly, there are new stakes to the story.* By putting pressure on John to save his daughter and abandon the quest to save the world, we now have a twist that re-engages the reader into the storyline. He has to choose between two Primal Instincts – survival of the world, or saving his daughter. And only one is more noble. Therefore, when he chooses his daughter, he becomes more heroic. Now, of course, he could have also sacrificed his daughter (but we'll get to that element in a second), but that would make him less heroic.

The technique of reaching beyond the main storyline to find those fringe elements and using them to exert pressure into the story is called **Peripheral Plotting**. The creator could have used a stranger off the street and threatened their lives - but this wouldn't have been personal to John, and therefore wouldn't have touched our hearts. He could have decided to threaten the life of the president, but this is too far out of the periphery for John. Peripheral Plotting requires that the plot element be *Personal* and close in *Proximity*.

Another great example of Peripheral Plotting is the television show *24*. Notice how, at any given point, Jack Bauer has two or three other issues to deal with, on a personal level, along with saving the world? In the last season I saw, Jack was trying to find a terrorist (of course) who was trying to keep the president from sending troops into an African country. This is a noble goal, but it doesn't touch Jack's life, unless you saw the prequel, where Jack is in the African country and sees his friends killed. As the season opens, Jack is standing trial for his many "crimes" but is pulled away because of his personal knowledge of the situation. (Why!) As we get further into the story, Peripheral Stakes begin to weave into the story. Suddenly, Jack discovers he must save his best friend from being sucked into a terrorist plot. Then, he is required to save the president's life and another friend is killed. Then, Jack contracts a biological disease and is going to die, which brings his estranged daughter into the scene. When she is threatened, he'll do anything to save her. The gem of this plotting is that all of these things are happening at the same time, making it harder for him to complete the big picture task.

All of these conspire to raise the stakes and keep the adrenaline flowing in the story.

*How do you find those Peripheral Stakes?*
Look around you – each one of us has people and things we care about in a widening circle. This is our periphery.

Let's say my goal is to get to the airport so I can get to Seattle to see my mother for Christmas. In a linear plot, all that might stand between me and my goal might be transportation, or perhaps money. Maybe getting time off from my job. But let's do some peripheral plotting.

Let's say that I get a call from the principle of the school. My son has had a fight on the playground and they can't find his father (who is supposed to pick him up). I must get off work early and go to the school. Now, my son has been pulled in from the periphery.

After meeting with the principle, I call my husband and discover that he never showed up at work today. Let's add more stress to the plot and say that we are estranged. Now, do I go find him, or do I drop my son off at my sister's house? In plotting, I could pull in the disappearance of my estranged husband into the periphery.

But let's say that I decide to ignore him, and head home to get my bags and drop my son off. When I get home, I discover that my house has been broken into. I must call the police, and one of the answering officers just happens to be an old boyfriend I haven't seen in years.

Now I have two more peripheral elements – the ransacked house and the old beau.

See how the story is widened already?

Now, a missed call and cryptic message on my cell phone from someone I don't know, but who says she knows where my missing ex-husband is, pulls in another element and raises the stakes even more. Especially when I convince the old beau to come with me to meet this woman…and find her dead!

See how pulling in peripheral events suddenly creates more tension? I might then also turn the focus back onto the main goal by having my mother call, and tell me she is on her way to the hospital with chest pains.

Now, this is an intriguing story.

**Book Therapist Question:** As you're plotting, ask: What is the worst thing (within reason) that could happen, right now, to someone or something in your periphery that would derail your own quest in life?

Another way to figure out peripheral stakes is to do **Visual Plotting**: Create an idea web, with your character at the center, and a web of the things he or she cares about around that central hub. Then it's easy to see the big picture and create scenarios or "what-ifs" for each of these things. From there, you can develop the Peripheral Stakes. (I often use Inspiration Software, a brainstorming program, to gather my thoughts.)

*Note:* Peripheral Stakes are *not* Subplots, or even layers, but additional devices used in the main storyline. But, peripheral plotting can help you find those layers or Subplots you may want to incorporate into the story. (We'll talk about Subplots and layers next!)

*Pick someone or something in your character's periphery and create trouble.* Something that could potentially divert your hero's attention, or even damage him. As he races to solve this peripheral problem, of course, the larger stake is affected, and worsens. He is forced to choose between two equally good Primal Instincts and your reader is on the edge of their seat.

*Finding Peripheral Stakes opens up new scenes, new secondary characters, new plotlines and new opportunities for character growth and widens your plot!*

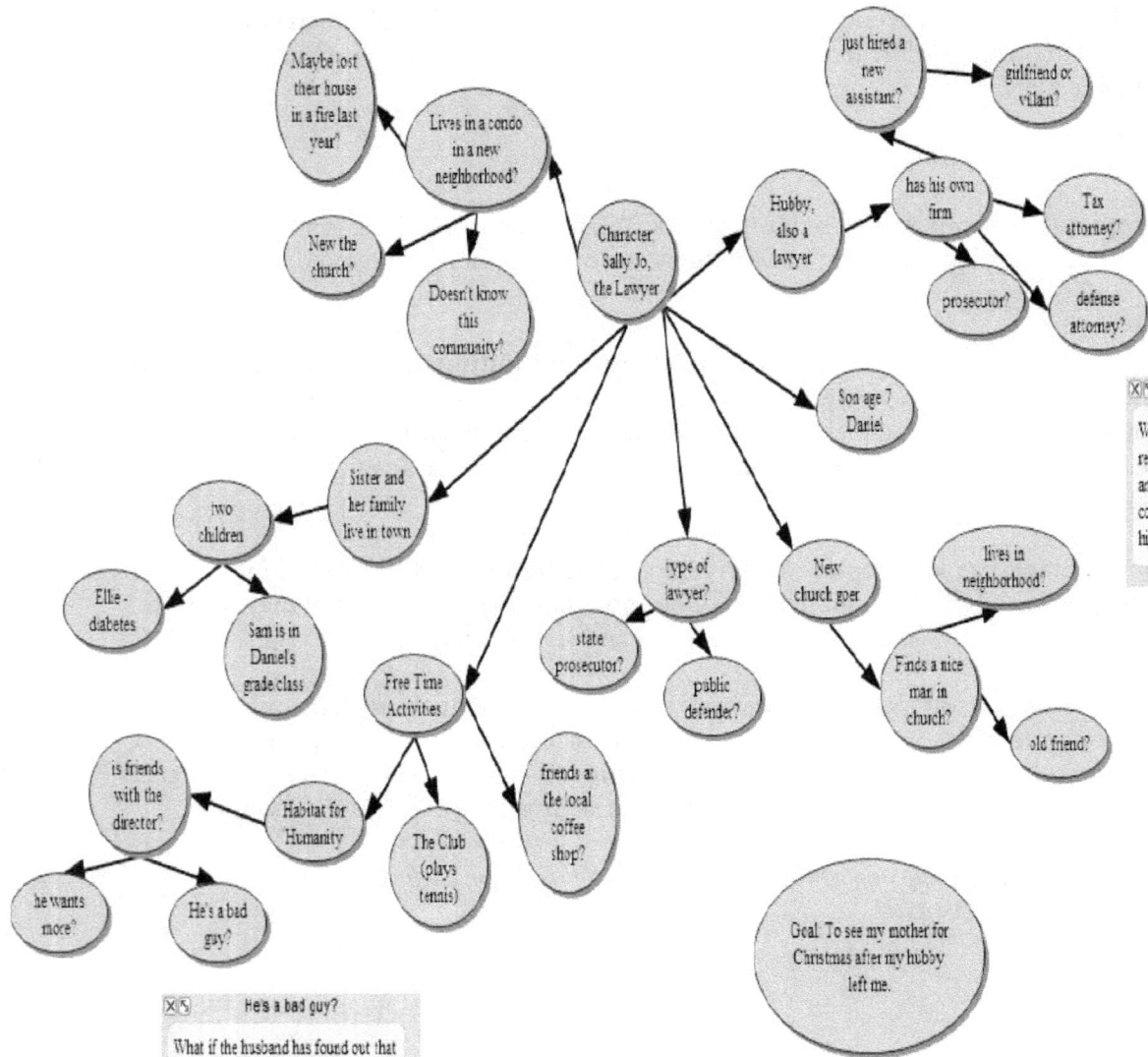

**Make Your Plot Wider:**

What is in your character's periphery?

- ✓ Create an Idea web, with your character in the middle.

- ✓ Create their world, with all the possibilities that come to mind. Include friends, activities, family, job – even enemies.

- ✓ Now, pick one element in that periphery and cause some trouble.
  (And if you want – don't stop there!)

## Subplots and Layers

Now that you've figured out the big picture Why and Why not, added heroism and Peripheral Stakes and put them together in the right balance to drive the plot, let's expand your plot further, and really give the theme resonance.

When you're working with plot, you want something that lingers in your readers mind – makes an impact, regardless if it's suspense, or romance or women's fiction. One of the key elements to making your plot WIDER is adding **Subplots** and **Layers.**

*We're going to talk first about the difference between the two, and then how to use them for powerful plotting and impact in a story.*

One of my favorite teeny-bop movies is *Chasing Liberty*. It's the story of an 18-year-old girl who is the president's daughter. She wants to attend the Berlin Love Parade, so she runs away from her parents while they are on a diplomatic tour in Europe. The president, aware of his daughter's mischief, assigns a Secret Service agent to watch over her and keep her out of trouble. The agent is a young, attractive man and of course, the daughter falls in love with him. His goal is to not fall in love with his assignment while keeping her safe.

By the way, it's a very loose remake of *Roman Holiday*. The difference is that the remake took the theme of "royal girl on vacation" to a new level by adding in a Subplot.

Embedded in this tale is another tale: the romance of two more Secret Service agents tracking the above-mentioned duo. Their story is what makes this movie such a delight – their banter, their eventual romance, their happy ending. It's this extra story in a story that that gives the movie the sparkle that takes it from teeny-bop to good-enough-for-grownups.

**In short, the Subplot makes the movie.**

**What is the difference between a *Subplot* and a *Story layer?***

**A Story Layer** is an element to the plot that adds depth and enhances the character struggle and eventually his/her epiphany. **A Story Layer deepens the *theme* of the story.**

A layer is some fringe element in the periphery that directly relates to the character growth, and thereby, the plot of the story. However, a layer, if standing alone would be lacking a story arc and its own three act plot.

For example, if you've read my book *Happily Ever After*, you know that Joe, our hero, has a brother, Gabe, who has Down syndrome. Joe is in town to reconnect with his brother – and part of the story is how they accomplish this. But there is no Black Moment between them, no character arc for Gabe. It's just a layering tool used to reveal Joe's insecurities, his issues with unforgiveness, and to give Joe a glimpse at what unconditional love looks like. And all these elements feed back into the main plot – Joe's inability to commit to a relationship with the heroine, Mona.

**A Subplot, however, is its own distinct story.** It has an Inciting Incident, obstacles, a Black Moment, and lessons learned (and hopefully a happily ever after). A Subplot can mirror the main plot, and even intersect with it, but it has its own main characters, its own arc, and if pulled out of the story, could stand alone as a mini-story.

Subplots are often found in longer books, due to the extra word count needed to form a complete story. Layers are found in shorter books and used to enhance the main plot.

*Let's consider some examples from movies:*
In *How to Lose a Guy in 10 Days* is the roommate's romance a Subplot or a layer? (Layer) It starts with the Black Moment, and all we see is the happy ending. It isn't its own story.

In *The Patriot* is Gabriel's romance a Subplot or layer? (Subplot) Gabriel meets his girl, dates her, they have obstacles (their past), overcome them, have a wedding, and she dies and it changes his life.

In *Independence Day* there is a Subplot *and* a layer: The romance with Captain Steven Hiller (Will Smith) is a Subplot, the one with David Levinson (Jeff Goldblum) is a layer.

Captain Hiller and his girl, Jasmine, have an Inciting Incident (he has to leave to go back to work on the 4th of July), an obstacle, (he wants to marry her, but her background as a stripper stands in the way of his career goals of being an astronaut), a Black Moment (he left her behind and the city is destroyed) and an Epiphany (he doesn't want to lose her). When he finds her, he realizes what is important, proposes, and they find happiness, which gives him the strength to be the astronaut he's always wanted to be.

David Levinson has never given up on his marriage, even though he's divorced. The few moments he has with his wife reveals that they need to focus on the important things – that they still love each other – to get through this. This is a strong layer, but with no Black Moment, no full story arc. Can you see the difference?

In *Return to Me,* is the romance between the waitress and the cook a Subplot or a Story Layer? (Layer)
In the *Pirates of the Caribbean* is the romance of Will and Elizabeth a Subplot or a layer? That should be obvious.

Most movies have layers because Subplots take up more time. Shorter books require layers instead of Subplots. Longer books, and certain genres, like Women's Fiction or Long Romance can have Subplots.

Let's analyze some of my books:
- *Happily Ever After* has a layer with Gabe, Joe's brother.
- *The Perfect Match* has a layer with Joe and Mona losing a child.
- *Wiser than Serpents* has a Subplot with Gracie and Vicktor.
- The Team Hope series has a layer threaded throughout with Sarah and Hank
- *Reclaiming Nick* has a Subplot with Cole and Maggie.
- *Taming Rafe* has two Subplots – one with Lolly and John, and yet another with the characters in John's novel.
- *Finding Stefanie* has a Subplot with Gabe and Libby.
- *Nothing but Trouble* has a story layer with PJ's nephew Davy

Remember – a Subplot stands alone and yet is connected to the story through theme and players. A layer simply accentuates the story theme.

**Adding in a Subplot or a layer will take your story wider, give it more breadth, as well as resonance.**

Layers are easy to build into a story – you just have to remember the two rules:

1. **Simplicity**
   The key to a great layer is focus. You don't want to make the message complicated but, rather, deepen it. First, *define your theme.* Forgiveness? Hope? Starting over?

   Now, *what do you want to say about it?* That you must forgive yourself before you can love another? That a second chance shouldn't be wasted? That hope is about looking past your present circumstances to the God who loves you?

   Finally ask: *Is there a character in the periphery* who can speak into the life of the character about it, either verbally, or through actions, or even through like circumstances?

   Maybe it's a friend, or a co worker, or a sibling, even a situation observable by the POV character.

In *Happily Ever After*, I used Gabe, Joe's brother, to model what forgiveness looked like to Joe.

In *The Perfect Match*, I used Joe and Mona's miscarriage and adoption of three children to illustrate that God is always at work behind the scenes of our lives. Joe and Mona were simply characters she knew in the community, but Joe served on the volunteer fire department and, thereby were people she could observe.

In *How to Lose a Guy in 10 Days*, the roommate provides the simple theme through her actions that perhaps we can do everything "wrong" and it can still be "right."

In *Return to Me*, the waitress and the cook provide the theme that two hearts that belong together can't be kept apart, and speak that truth in various ways to the hero.

**Keep the theme simple, and speak it through someone in the periphery or cast of characters.**

2. **Relevance**
A Story Layer has to be something that relates to the main story theme.

It may have just an element of the entire theme.
For example, in *Happily Ever After*, the Gabriel layer speaks to the importance of forgiving others to maintain family relationships. However, that is only one aspect of the forgiveness theme in the book. The entire forgiveness theme also takes a look at forgiving oneself as well as the ailments of unforgiveness.

Or it may speak to more than one of the characters.
In *The Perfect Match* both Ellie and Pastor Dan are dealing with their frustration at being unable to 'control' circumstances. Pastor Dan is afraid of getting involved with someone whom he could lose, Ellie believes that if she is "good" enough, she can keep bad things from happening. Watching Joe and Mona lose their child speaks to the frailty of that belief, yet seeing them adopt three orphaned children shows them both that God protects and provides in amazing ways. It speaks in two different ways to the theme.

Finally, a layer might add an ancillary thought that builds on the main theme.
In *Nothing but Trouble*, PJ Sugar is asked to take care of her nephew, Davy. Davy feels abandoned, and lashes out at PJ, afraid of her. It isn't until she takes him swimming, staying with him as he goes into the deep waters that they bond. PJ meanwhile feels as though she is a misfit, and unloved. That incident, which is similar to one she had with her mother as a child, starts to unlock the idea that perhaps she needs to start looking at her relationship with her mother differently. Maybe her mother also stuck with her, believed in her over the years, and that she loves her. The Davy layer is the spark that ignites PJ's revelation of the theme that God loves her.
*A relevant and simple story layer will widen your plot and deepen your theme.*

### *How do you build a Subplot?*

I admit that I love the television series *ER* and *Grey's Anatomy*. Because, as we all know, they are really big long soap operas. *Grey's* is, essentially, the on-again, off-again, hopefully on-again romance of Dr. Derrick McDreamy and Dr. Meredith Grey. Inside all this romance are the daily (read: episodic) events of a hospital in Seattle.

What makes *Grey's* interesting are the running monologues of the lead heroine, the thematic nuances she puts into the story, usually centered around the events of the episode, but also alluding to her current state of relationship with Derrick. One could say that the episode theme relates to the overall story arc of the series.

*Episodes in a soap-opera show like Grey's Anatomy act as Subplots to the main story.* They match the Subplot definition: *Short but concise stories that reveal theme and, taken alone, would stand on their own merit.*

**Let's take one of my favorites episodes: The Bomb in the Body.** (Also has Kyle Chandler, the *Friday Night Lights* guy (formerly *Early Edition*) guest starring, and I just love him).

The Subplot starts with the inciting incident – a man comes in with a hole in his stomach. A paramedic is putting pressure against the bleeding – *inside his body*. The conflict is if she takes her hand out, he'll bleed to death. So, the doctors take them up to surgery. The stakes are raised when his wife arrives and reveals that the man was playing with a bazooka – *There is an unexploded bomb in his body*. The paramedic freaks out, pulls her hand from his body, wherein Dr. Grey takes her place.

Of course, Dr. Grey is doomed, and the rest of the show is her wishing that she could turn back time and rethink where she is right now.

Meanwhile, in the *big* plot, Derrick and Dr. Grey have had an affair, and she's in love with him. Unfortunately, she didn't know he was married until just a few weeks prior when Derrick's *wife* (Cue the dramatic background music, please!) showed up.

Derrick wants a divorce…he thinks. But, maybe not, so he decides to give his marriage another chance. Meredith's heart is broken. She wishes she could turn back time and rethink her life. See the parallel?

Of course, they get the bomb out of the body, and sadly, as cute Kyle walks away with it, it blows up. He's vaporized. And Meredith is left with blood all over her, a casualty of another person's error in judgment. Of course, the patient who wreaked all this havoc, lives.

Again, see the parallel to the main story arc?

**A great Subplot is about mirroring the theme of the main plot.** It can either enhance it – e.g., show what could happen if one choice is made, or put it in relief – show what will happen if that choice *isn't* made. The Subplot can act be a testing ground for "what if."

I've had a lot of fun with recent Subplots. The biggest Subplot I ever used was the Subplot within a Subplot I put into *Taming Rafe* – a love story written by one of the characters (John) that reveals the feelings the character has for a woman he's never declared his love to (Lolly), written via the romance of the characters in *his* book, a book that the POV characters in *Taming Rafe* all read. (Okay, did that make sense? Basically, it's a story within a story). A Subplot widens the story and increases the stakes on many different fronts so that the reader is invested not just in the main storyline, but all of them.

In *Finding Stefanie,* I used the young romance of a former gang-banger to reveal how a little faith in someone can change a person's entire life. We not only care about Gideon and Libby, but I use the theme to show the hero how his life might be affected if he allows himself to have faith in Stefanie.

**As you're developing your Subplot first ask: What lesson will the characters in my main plot learn?** Is there a smaller lesson, or a piece of that lesson I can illuminate through the Subplot? Remember, the Subplot doesn't have to be directly connected to the main plot to be effective – yes, it should affect the main plot in some way, but it also stands on its own.

**Then look at your peripheral plotting web and ask: Who is the best person to illustrate that story, either through a bad choice or a good choice?**

Remember, also, a Subplot has to have all the elements of a story: Inciting incident, conflict, Black Moment, Epiphany and a climatic ending.

**When do you start the Subplot?**

A good Subplot starts after the main plot is established. Usually, I begin the Subplot after I've introduced the main characters and their conflict, often about three chapters in. Then, to keep it flowing, I usually put in one Subplot scene or POV per every four to five main povs. That way I keep the Subplot flowing without overwhelming the main plot. Finally, I tie up the Subplot at least three chapters before the main story ends.

Creating a Subplot for your book is much like creating a main plot – you must figure out your character, and their fear and dreams and goals. However, you only have to stick to the main elements. Don't worry about the emotional journey, or even the unlayering – keep it simple, but focused on illuminating the main theme of the plot.

### How do you decide between a Subplot or a Layer?

The answer lies in both the plot scope and the story length. Do you need more action and depth to your main story? If your story is not high action, or the plot not complicated, or even if you have a highly technical plot, you may need a Subplot to deep your story.

If your story is already filled with twists and turns, with a large cast, and a technical plot, then a Story Layer is a better fit. You'll want to accentuate the main plot instead of draw attention from it and engage the reader in another.

Another consideration is word count. Do you have enough room in the actual word count to build in a Subplot? A mass market book, like Heartsong or Steeple Hill Love Inspired, or even any of the other mass market lines might not have enough room in their word count to allow for a full-out Subplot. More than that (check with your editors), many of the mass market lines prefer a simple hero-heroine structure.

However, if you have a trade-sized book with 90-100k word count, you probably have room to build in a solid but tight Subplot.

Whether you use a Subplot or a layer, incorporating one or the other will widen your plot and help you create a book that makes an impact on your reader.

**Widen your Plot:**

✓ Consider the kind of book you are writing – is it better suited for a Subplot or a layer?

✓ What is the theme of your story?

✓ What would you like to accentuate, add to, or spark in relationship to that theme?

✓ Look into your character's periphery. Who could you use to create a Story Layer or plot?

✓ If you are creating a Story Layer, name one key scene you will use to accentuate that layer.

✓ If you are creating a story Subplot, plot out the mini story arc:

- Inciting Incident

- Obstacle/Conflict

- Black Moment

- Epiphany (Lesson Learned)

- Happy ending/Application by the POV characters (Main plot)

## *How to use Secondary Characters for maximum effect*

I love football. From August to February, our family is glued to Sunday afternoon football (and Monday, and Thursday, and the occasional Saturday). Football is a true team sport. Everyone must be playing their positions in order for the team to score or defend. My sons play football, and we often talk about how they can play in their position, how a touchdown for one is a touchdown for all.

Sure, the QB is the main character. The wide receivers and running backs principle players. Tackles and Guards and Ends are secondary players, although equally important to the entire picture.

A good story is set up like a football game. (Maybe that's why I like it!) You have the Main Character, the principle characters who push the plot forward, and then you have the defenders – those secondary players who deliver information, or add resonance to the layer, or even provide the Subplot.

A Secondary Character doesn't have to just be a place marker, the guy who serves coffee or the waitress at the café, or the nosy neighbor. A Secondary Character can widen the plot even further by giving them a Voice of Reason…or Passion.

**The Voice of Reason or Passion**

The Voice of Passion lives in my house. She's dressed like my teenage daughter (on any given day that might be a pair of jeans, topped with a skirt, with a tank top under a short-sleeved sweatshirt, and a pair of what my husband calls, her "Wonder Woman" arm protectors).

Now, to be fair, my daughter has long moments of reason, where sanity prevails. Moment when I am able to convince her that no, her brothers aren't trying to drive her crazy, even though they insist on leaving the bathroom…well, you know. In these moments, I glimpse the woman that she will be, and know that truth does make it way inside.

And then there are the moments when passion takes over. When, despite her best efforts, life is simply too much. In these moments, she must play her music at the top of the allowed decibel levels and, to put into *Grey's Anatomy Speak*, she has to dance it out. In these moments, that inner wild thing must be heard and set free. Only then can she breathe deeply, and eventually find reason again.

Sadly, or perhaps comfortingly, I see so much of myself in her. So, I know, someday, this too shall pass. (Or not, according to my husband).

So, the point is, we all have two sides to ourselves: a **Voice of Reason**, and a **Voice of Passion**.

117

Your character does too. As you develop your character, try asking: What, at the time of crisis, would your Voice of Reason tell you to do? And what would your Voice of Passion dictate you do? Knowing this allows you to apply these moments to their character change.

However, when dealing with Secondary Characters giving them their own particular **Voice** is a great way to illustrate the **Theme** of the story.

Let's say our theme is forgiveness, as in *Happily Ever After*. Joe is grappling with forgiveness, and doesn't know how to forgive someone for something that happened to him. Gabe, his brother, acts as the layer, illustrating what forgiveness looks like. Gabe also acts as a Voice of Reason, the voice that has perspective and grace and has found the right answer.

Also in the story is a villain, someone who is out to sabotage the heroine, Mona. The villain is acting out of *unforgiveness*, and his anger is causing him to lose his morals, and eventually his freedom. The villain is the Voice of Passion – unforgiveness out of control.

Another example is *The Hunt for Red October*. Of course, the central character in the theme is Jack Ryan and the theme is loyalty and trust. Of course, our Voice of Reason is the Russian Sub Commander (Sean Connery), who has looked at his life and this silent war and decided to aim for the US Eastern Seaboard. In the end, he decides to trust someone he's never met. The Voice of Passion is the *other* Russian sub commander, who decides *not* to trust his own countrymen, and in fact kill them. But it's two sides to the same theme: How much should you trust someone?

The Voice of Reason and the Voice of Passion are great ways to utilize your Secondary Characters. The key is to look for ways you can accentuate the theme, to give it different points of view, and then apply them to your Secondary Characters.

**Ask: What is my theme?**

**Then ask: What would the Voice of Reason do with my theme?**
Look around your cast of characters. Is there anyone who can act as the Voice of Reason?

Likewise ask: How would the Voice of Passion react to my theme? Is there a character who could act as the Voice of Passion? Perhaps in a moment of fear, or a moment of darkness? It could be friend of the hero who makes a poor decision. Or a villain who takes the theme the other way?

The answers to these questions work to widen your plot as they surface new scenes to insert into your story.

The key isn't to have the Voice of Reason have a "Reason Conversation" with your hero or heroine. It's to illustrate for the *reader* the two sides of the theme with key scenes.

You may want to insert a scene of Reason or Passion at the beginning of the story (e.g. the roommate in *How to Lose a Guy in 10 Days* is the Voice of Passion, and is inserted as the Inciting Incident at the beginning of the movie.)

Or, you can insert a Voice of Passion/Reason scene in the middle, during a moment of contemplation by the hero. It can even be in memory. (e.g. in *P.S. I Love You,* the heroine remembers how her husband dared her to sing karaoke, and out of anger (passion) she took the bet, and fell and broke her nose. She never forgave him. Until the Voice of Reason allow her to sing again, this time with a right heart, and she was able to heal the memory of hurting her husband).

Or perhaps a scene at the end, during the climatic moments. (e.g. during the fight scene between the submarines in *The Hunt for Red October*, the Russian sub commander who is hunting the Red October plays it safe (Reason) and doesn't arm his missiles in time to destroy the Red October. The Voice of Passion then takes over, he arms his missiles, and ultimately…blows up his own sub).

When you apply the Voice of Reason and Passion to your story, suddenly your Secondary Characters aren't simply placeholders, but important players on the storytelling team.

**Widen your Plot:**

✓ What is your story theme?

✓ What would the Voice of Reason do with your theme?

✓ How would the Voice of Passion react to your theme?

✓ Pick two Secondary Characters in your cast.

✓ What does the Voice of Reason Character do to show….Reason?

✓ What does the Voice of Passion Character do to show…Passion?

✓ What two new scenes can you write into your plot to widen it with these Voices?

    Scene #1

    Scene #2

## The One Key Scene Every Book Should Have!

Every book needs the *one thing your character would never do* scene.

Think back to the layering section of our Character Deepening section. In Layer Four's reveal, your character begins to have *out of character behavior. In this phase of layering, you are putting him into situations that confront his fears, and forcing him to reveal his dreams, to the heroine, or to the reader, almost like turning the crank on a vice to make him open himself up.*

*In the last part of that section,* **he then reveals himself** *through the* **Sacrificial Act.** *The sacrificial act is found by asking:* What would your character never do? And then follow up with the question: What would make him do it?)

**You must put this scene into your plot.**

You know your character well enough by now to understand what he'd never do. The scene that must be included in your story, and your plot, is when he does it.

Rafe (*Taming Rafe*) would never turn his back on bull riding and his accomplishments. Not when it is the only thing he believes gives him value. *Unless* he believes that it doesn't matter how much he's worked for, it's all gone. In that moment, he might even despise his past, and all that he worked for that netted him nothing.

So, in a scene that exemplifies this, Rafe burns everything he's worked so hard for.

Frodo would *never* put on the ring. Never dare to keep it. Unless he was forced to choose between his beloved ring and destroying it. The ring had quietly wooed him by making him unique and powerful, and the adventurer he had always wondered if he could be. So, in powerful, heart-wrenching scene, Frodo does what he would never do and must have the ring wrestled from him by Gollum.

**What would your character never do, and happens when he does it?** This scene completes the character journey, and makes for a powerful moment when the reader realizes just how far the hero has come, and how much he's changed.

The key element of this scene is Sacrifice. We touched on it in the Character Layer section, but ultimately, the character needs to sacrifice that which is holding him back from a final change, even sacrifice that which is holding him back from love. **Ask: What can you character sacrifice in that One Thing Moment?**

The Sacrifice is that element in the scene that will make your plot stick with your reader.

**Make your Plot Wider:**

- ✓ What is the one thing that your character would never do?

- ✓ What would make him do it?

- ✓ What can your character sacrifice in the One Thing Moment?

- ✓ Can you see the scene? Brainstorm it out.

# Villains

Any talk of plot widening has to include a great villain. I believe a villain is anyone or anything that seeks to destroy another person's confidence, goals – even their hope. A villain chews at a person's competence, raining upon them doubt, stirring up their fears and leaves them helpless.

A villain, really, can be anything – a past nightmare coming to life, a physical limitation, a natural disaster, an animal (remember Cujo?) and most importantly a personal attack from someone intent on hurting you. It can be circumstances, or even…yourself. Yes, I am so often my own worst enemy, my own personal villain. I set up goals for myself, and when I don't reach them (thanks to all the other goals I set up) I rain down doubt, frustration and disappointment on myself. I set my own traps to failure when I schedule in too many things, or set my bar so high it's unreachable. I even sharpen my tongue against myself. Yes, you know what I'm talking about.

All these elements can be used as villains in your story. Think of the tornados in *Twister*, and the ocean in *The Perfect Storm*. Powerful Villains.

How about a physical limitation? Remember *Seabiscuit?* That movie about a winning horse and jockey during the Great Depression? Both of them are injured – their physical limitations serve as the villain in the story.

Perhaps the villain is someone loveable and unintentional – like Marley the dog in *Marley and Me*. Or even your own issues, like the character in *Click,* who didn't like stress and fast-forwarded through his life.

For me, the scariest villain I've ever encountered would have to be, hands down, Alan Rickman, all the way across the board. Remember him? *Die Hard* – Hans Gruber (the mastermind thief), *Robin Hood: Prince of Thieves* – the Sheriff of Nottingham (Ewww!), the Harry Potter series – Severus Snape. I know he's played a few good guys but the guy embodies *bad* so well, I just love to watch him. Why? Because he makes you believe he's bad. We know he's out of his mind and crazy, and we don't know what to expect except….*badness.*

But it's not just his badness that makes him, um, bad. Alan Rickman's characters embody the four key elements to building the kind of villain, whether human or otherwise, that will contribute to widening the plot of your book.

## "Don't shoot, I believe you!"

**The first component to creating a villain is Believability.** We, as the reader (and the hero) have to believe that the Villain is truly….villainous. We have to believe in our hearts that what he threatens will occur.

The storm will sink the ship. The tornado will destroy the house. The dog will swallow the priceless necklace. A person's inabilities will keep him from accomplishing his goals. A killer will find your heroine and kill her.

We need to believe the threat of the villain.

But wait, you say, what about a suspense or mystery where we don't know who the villain even *is* until the end? How can we believe the threats of someone we haven't met?

Believing a villain is not about looking at the villain and measuring him up *It's about the damage it/he/she leaves behind. Think:* **Results.** A villain isn't a villain based on what he says about himself…but what he *does*.

If you want to create believablity for your villain, make him/her/it do something villainous in the beginning to drive that belief home. Show him in action, or show us his handiwork.

In the movie *Dante's Peak*, the villain is the volcano. To prove the believability of this threat, the movie opens with our hero trying to outrun another volcano – only to have his sweetheart, in the car next to him, die from a lava ball. We know, then, when our hero encounters another volcano awakening, it means business and can kill.

In *Twister,* the movie opens with….a twister. And the death of the heroine's father.

In *Marley and Me*, the voice of the narrator opens the story with his memory of the perfect dog, and the ominous prediction that Marley isn't it.

When the hero is his own worst enemy, begin the novel with a glimpse at how he self-sabotages. We want to see the foibles.

And of course, with an in-the-flesh villain, we need to just how bad he is. Hence the dead bodies at the beginning of thrillers and suspense books.

**Ask: What scene can you insert at the beginning of your book to prove to the reader that your villain's threat is believable?**

Believability = Alan Rickman = Please leave the lights on. (I'll be up all night reading anyway).

## Why pick on me?

I had a grade school villain. Her name was Karla, and she, like most bullies, had been held back a year in school and seemed as if she came out of the womb fully grown. She had a gang – her little brother and a few other cling-ons who were fed by her power. She and her gang owned the swings.

I love to swing. Especially the old kind of swings that hang from chains. In our playground, we could tie one of the set of three to the side, and then play a game with the other two. The "swinger" in the middle would swing in a circle, gathering momentum. At the exact right moment, the other "swinger" would position themselves in the middle and the two swings would join and knot together, twirling both gleeful playground swingers in a tight circle. I loved it, and I was good at it.

And Karla didn't like that.

Sometimes, she'd get to the swing before me, and she and her gang would just hang around the swings the entire recess. Taunting. *Not* swinging. Stealing all the swings from us innocent joyriders. Occasionally, they'd even use their fear tactics to force *me* off the swings. I hated that she had this power, that she could command this fear inside of me, and make it do her bidding.

It felt very, very personal.

So, one day I stood my ground as she and her scoundrels surrounded me. I wouldn't budge, and one of them held my hands behind my back, because Karla was going to punch me. The worst part was that I let them! I thought, *Oh, it's inevitable. I'm going to have to take my beating because I stood up to the Great Karla.*

I snapped. I was angry and tired of her picking on me – so I did what all fourth graders do. I cried. Then, I screamed, and broke free from my imprisoners and launched myself at Karla. She pushed me away, and at that moment, the 'Duty' came running up and saved us all (probably me) from bloodshed.

We stood in line to go to class, and her group laughed at me as I wiped the tears from my face, and tried to hide the scratches on my legs. But after that day, she veered clear of me on the swings.

I told this story years later to a classmate and she laughed (we both did). But her words stuck with me. "Oh, Karla didn't scare me because I didn't play on the swings. She didn't even care that I existed. But you lived in her neighborhood." Her words hit me like a gong. Karla rode my bus and who knows in how many ways I had personally annoyed her. (And what's wrong with singing Karen Carpenter at the top of your lungs on the way to school I ask?) I had somehow made myself a target for Karla, and she became my villain because it was **Personal.**

**The second element of a great Villain is one who makes it Personal.**

Even if it's a global villain, like a nuclear war, it has to touch the life of the hero or heroine in a *personal way.*

In *War of the Worlds*, although the entire family is affected by the aliens who want to suck their blood, it gets personal when Ray (Tom Cruise) and his daughter are stuck in the basement with a madman who just might give away their hiding place and get them all killed. The madman becomes a secondary villain in the story as he alerts the aliens to their presence. It's then that the aliens make it personal and decide to hunt down Ray and his daughter.

In *Dante's Peak*, the volcano eruption gets personal when the grandmother refuses to leave the mountain, and the children of the heroine go after her – only to get trapped in the lava. Although the act of nature isn't personal, it becomes personal when they're caught in the vortex of trauma and can't get free.

Remember the movie *Outbreak?* The villain here is a contagious disease (the Ebola virus). It gets personal when the doctor's ex-wife (whom he still loves) is infected. Now the story is about saving *her* instead of an entire town.

To create a powerful villain – whether it be nature, or circumstance, or human – have the villain zero in on your hero/heroine and hurt them (or threaten to hurt them) in a way that feels personal.

It gets personal in *The Patriot* when the British Colonel Tavington kills Benjamin Martin's son, burn his house and take his oldest son off to be hanged. It gets personal in *Lord of the Rings: The Fellowship if the Rings* when the Ringwraiths find Frodo and wound him on Weathertop. It gets personal in *The Fugitive* when Samuel Gerard (the US Marshal) tells Dr. Kimble that he doesn't care if he's innocent, he's just going to bring him in.

But, it's not only about making it Personal. The personal connection must be **Justified.** It must make sense.

In *Dante's Peak*, if the hero and heroine had simply gone on a picnic on the mountain, and gotten caught it in the lava flow, it wouldn't have been justified. The hero is a man who understands that the volcano is about to blow. But, placing her mother (who is stubborn, an element that was established earlier) in the lava's path, and sending the children to rescue her (which then brings the hero and heroine to the lava's path) justifies the personal connection to the threat.

In *The Patriot,* the threat becomes personal because Gabriel is wounded while carrying a messenger bag, and comes to his father's home for help. The war is nearby and Benjamin Martin's front porch becomes a makeshift hospital for both British and American forces. However, Gabriel's actions bring Tavington and his men to Martin's door, and his younger son's impulsiveness at Gabriel's arrest ignites the personal war between Martin and Tavington. The personal threat is justified.

**Ask:** How can you make the threat Personal *and* Justified?

Then, add in a scene that shows why or how it becomes Personal.

One way to show how Personal it can get is to give a hint to how it might become Personal.

For example, if I were writing this as a novel, I might show how Karla had beaten up the first Queen of the Swings, and thus that she would do the same to me. Or, if I truly had annoyed her on the bus, I might show that scene of me innocently singing a la Karen Carpenter, and Karla's silent rage (probably that she had always wanted to be an amazing KC singer).

You can often build in the believability and the foreshadowing of the personal, justified nature of the threat in the same scene. Like *Dante's Peak's* prologue scene with the death of the hero's girlfriend by a lava rock. In that scene, we see both the Believability and the personal threat of the volcano, for our hero.

Frodo's wounding on Weathertop also combings the Believability and personal threat of the Ringwraiths in Lord of the Rings.

But making the threat **Believable** and **Personal** are only the first two elements of creating a plot-widening villain.

### I'll Get You, My Pretty!

One of my favorite villains of all time is the Wicked Witch of the West. I used to lie in bed after *The Wizard of Oz* every year, listening to the witch cackle in my mind and tremble. I even knew a lady who *looked* like the witch and every time she came near me I went running.

What made the witch so scary? Well, first she was Believable – she rode in on a broomstick and terrified the Munchkins. And then it got Personal (I'll get you, My Pretty, and your little dog too!) And then....she seemed to be **Unbeatable.** She could see in her little crystal ball what Dorothy was doing, and she had those scary flying monkeys, and most of all, we knew she wanted those red slippers – a goal that was equal to Dorothy's goal of getting home. Her powers were bigger than Dorothy's, and it seemed she was out-thinking our singing heroine, and she even ambushed her (in a field of poppies).

A great villain, whether it be something inside us, an external force, or a green witch chasing us down a yellow road has to be seemingly Unbeatable. It must be bigger than him, or stronger than him, it must be able to out-think the hero, and even lay in wait to ambush him. In other words, the villain must have powers *equal* or *greater than* the hero.

Benjamin Martin's guerilla tactics are matched and topped by Col. Tavington's brutality. And when Tavington traps an entire village in a church and burns it to the ground, he seems unbeatable.

Sauron's ability to find Frodo through the Ringwraiths and even Gollum keeps the viewers always on edge. No, Frodo, don't put on the ring!

It's the ultra-hot lava burning everything in its path.

It's the perfect storm, taking down a coastguard helicopter.

It's the US Marshals, capturing the other escapee from the wrecked train in *The Fugitive*.

For every Why that proves your character is the perfect hero for his journey, the Villain has a Why Not that is just as strong or stronger. And, as you're plotting, find that unbeatable element you can hold over your hero.

**Here's How:** Go back to your hero's competence, those elements in the Why of the journey. Now ask: What could defeat him and how?

In *Dante's Peak,* the hero's competence is his ability to read the volcano's moods and predict when it will blow. But what if it blows too early? What if he hasn't been able to adequately prepare? And this element, coupled with the inevitable unstoppability of the lava makes the volcano unbeatable.

In *The Fugitive*, the hero's competence is about believing his innocence, and knowing how to solve the crime. But he's *not* a criminal, and he hasn't spent his life trying to outrun the law. He simply doesn't have the skills he needs to stay away from the US Marshals forever. And his desperation might make him reckless. So, the fear of a mistake combined with the US Marshal's reputation that he always gets his man makes the villain unbeatable.

Your villain must always be one step ahead of your hero, or more brutal than your hero, or stronger, or better armed, or better financed, or have a larger army, or have superpowers…anything that makes him unbeatable.

Until… the hero finds their weakness.

Pitted against the villain, the goal of the hero becomes to find the villain's weakness, (even if it's a pot of water (I'm melting, I'm melting!)) and defeat the enemy.

## And you're little dog, too!

Your villain's threat is Believable, Personal, and Unbeatable…and now the key to a great villain is that they must understand the hero or heroine's greatest **Tangible fear**.

For a villain to be great, his or her threats must be believable and truly scary…and it must hit home. In *The Wizard of Oz*, we're afraid for Dorothy and her friends, but when the witch threatens Toto, we're drawn all the way into the danger. Dorothy has already gone after her little dog (that's why she's in the storm and not safely in the cellar), so we know she loves him, and her greatest fear is that he'll be taken.

Why is it not a hero or heroine's Greatest Fear? Because often their greatest fear has something to do with their past – losing someone they love, being lost or alone, perhaps even seeing everything taken from them. These are all the effect of their greatest Tangible fear happening.

What's the difference? Well, something physical has to happen in order for them to find themselves inside the Black Moment of their greatest fears. Usually, it's about hurting someone they care about (like Toto.)

The Greatest Fear of Harry Dalton, the scientist in *Dante's Peak* (if you haven't seen this movie, you'll have to now), is to not evacuate soon enough the people in the path of an erupting volcano. His greatest Tangible fear is that it would kill someone he loves, specifically the heroine, (who he's fallen for) Rachel Wando.

Making it Tangible is different than making it Personal. Making it Personal means the threat is going after the character in particular. Making it Tangible means the threat will hurt someone or something they value.

Tavington kills Benjamin Martin's oldest son, Gabriel in *The Patriot*.

In *The Fugitive*, it is that the US Marshal doesn't care about solving the murder, and by capturing Dr. Kimble, his wife will figuratively die all over again.

Frodo fights Gollum when he tries to kill Samwise on Mt. Mordor.

It's a matter of asking: How can the villain hurt the hero or heroine the most? How can he cause the hero's or heroine's greatest fear to come about?

Start with the hero's Greatest Fear, (which you discovered when you interview him in *From the Inside-Out*) and then put a face to it. One in the hero's periphery. (See how all these plotting elements work together?)

Once you have that face and that event, you'll have the climatic moment of terror for your hero. (Usually this occurs right before or right after the Black Moment, depending on what you want to do with that Tangible fear).

*So, how does having a Villain widen your plot? Let's count up your new scenes...*

One scene where the threat is Believable, often at the beginning of the book.

One moment where the threat is Personal and Justified (Can be combined with the above scene).

One moment where the villain seems Unbeatable.

One moment where the villain makes the fears Tangible by threatening that which his closest to your hero's heart.

*Create the right villain, internal or external, live or a force of nature and use it to widen your plot!*

**Make your Plot Wider:** Is your villain's threat:

- ✓ Believable? How?


- ✓ Personal and Justified? How?


- ✓ Unbeatable (with Powers Equal or Greater than the Hero?)


- ✓ Tangible

**Now, add in the Scenes to Widen your Plot:**

Do you have a scene where the threat is Believable?

How will you make the threats Personal and Justified (is it combined with the scene above?)

In which scene will your villain seem Unbeatable?

At what moment/scene does the villain make the fears Tangible by threatening that which his closest to your hero's heart?

## Encouragement from your Therapist

If you've plotted your book with *From the Inside-Out: discover, create and publish the novel in you*, then you have all the elements of a solid plot. But just for a moment, imagine your reader when they read the scene where your villain becomes Unbeatable. Or the scene where one of your Secondary characters does exactly what the hero was about to do in a fit of Passion. Or that scene that shows the reader exactly Why the hero is perfect for the journey. Or finally, the poignant scene where they do that one thing they never thought they'd ever do...

*How did the author think of that?*

They look up from their book, draw in a breath.

From beside them, their spouse rouses. *"Did you say something, honey?"*

*"No, no, go back to sleep."*

*"Are you turning off the light soon?"*

Nope.

A great story has two sides – Deep Characterization of a sympathetic hero, and a compelling, Wide, breathtaking Plot. Do you need to incorporate everything in the Wide section of Plotting? No. But I encourage you to ask yourself...do I need this scene? This Subplot? This villain?

And if you do, you'll know why and how to insert it.

At t he very least, as you are trying to figure out what kind of scenes you need to have in your stories, consider the kinds of scene that make your plot Wider.

*"Why are you so tired?"*

*"Oh, I went to bed at 4 a.m.! I just had to finish the book!"*

Happy Writing!
# Susan May Warren

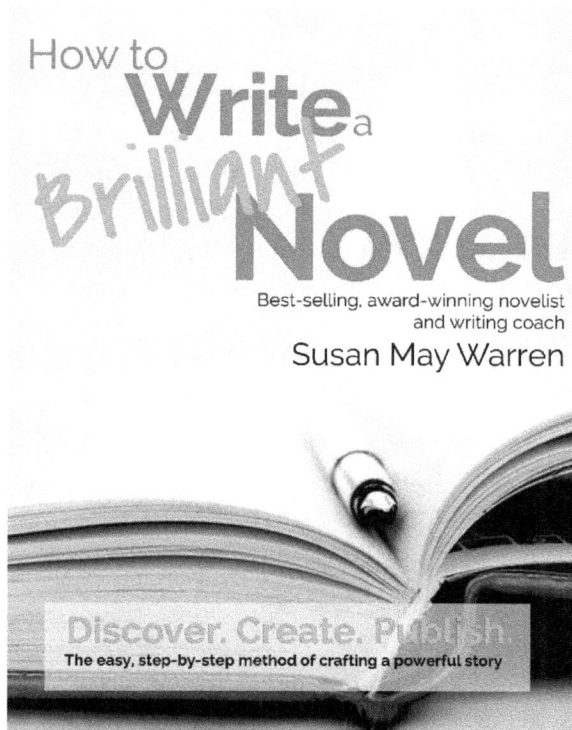

## How to Write a Brilliant Novel

The easy, step-by-step method of crafting a powerful story

What does it take to write a brilliant novel? Susan May Warren knows exactly how--and you're about to find out. She's coached hundreds of writers into publication, onto best-seller lists, and onto the awards platforms. (And she lives what she teaches. Susan is the bestselling author of over 50 novels, has won the Rita, the Christy, and the Carol awards multiple times.) Now, for the first time, she's revealing her step-by-step story crafting secrets that will show you how to discover, create, and publish the brilliant novel inside you.

## Susan's techniques are proven methods that will show you:

- Exactly how bestselling novels are designed

- How to create compelling characters

- How to construct tension-filled scenes. . .that keep readers devouring pagesHow to build sizzling dialogue

- How to develop riveting plots that keep readers guessingAnd once you're finished, how to sell your novel

### You CAN Write a Brilliant Novel!

"A quirky, fun, practical guide from a writer who knows what she's doing." -- James Scott Bell, bestselling author of *Write Great Fiction:Plot & Structure*.

# Advanced Brilliant Writing

**Best-selling, award-winning novelist and writing coach**

**Susan May Warren**

**Make your plot wider and your characters deeper.**

## Advanced Brilliant Writing

An amazing novel has two elements – deep characterization of a sympathetic hero, and a compelling, wide, breathtaking plot. But how do you create deep characters and wide plots and then apply them to your story? It's time to learn Advanced (Brilliant!) Writing. The follow-up to How to Write a Brilliant Novel, Advanced Brilliant Writing utilizes RITA and Christy award-winning, best-selling novelist Susan May Warren's easy to apply explanations, exercises and intuitive methods to teach you advanced fiction writing techniques that will turn any novel from boring to . . . brilliant.

**You'll learn:**

- How to plot a profound character change journey

- An easy technique to reveal backstory to your readers

- How to weave emotion into your scene for the most impact

- How to keep tension high through the use of stakes and motivations

- A unique plotting trick to widen your plot

- Techniques on how to make your hero…heroic

- The difference between subplots and layers

- A powerful use for Secondary characters

- How the perfect Villain can help you plot your story

**. . . and much more, including the scene that every book MUST have!**

"If you're intending to write a best-selling novel, I can think of no better place to start than with Susan May Warren's Deep and Wide. This is a book for those who need to dig into the techniques of writing -- not just hear the happy-talk, big-picture stuff that is so often heard at conferences. If you really want to get into the nuts and bolts of writing strong fiction, then this is for you. Clear, practical advice from an award-winning novelist." *Chip MacGregor, Literary Agent, MacGregor Literary*

# My Brilliant Book Buddy

**Best-selling, award-winning novelist and writing coach**

**Susan May Warren**

You've got a friend in me

The easy, step-by-step manuscript companion

## My Brilliant Book Buddy

The writing journey can be long and lonely. It's easy to get lost in the weeds of your story, not sure where you are headed . . . or why. Wouldn't it be nice to have a guide along the way? Someone to point you in the right direction, and keep you motivated.

A manuscript companion to the foundational writer's workbook How to Write a Brilliant Novel, and advanced writer's guide, Advanced Brilliant Writing, My Brilliant Book Buddy puts feet to all the steps needed to create a powerful book, guiding you through character creation, plotting the inner and outer journey, creating essential scenes, and word-painting. With step-by-step instruction, it helps you craft the perfect black moment, and pushes you on all the way to the climatic ending.

"The Book Buddy is my new best friend! It takes all of the helpful tools, charts and tips from Inside Out and Deep and Wide and puts them in one place. It's like having Susan May Warren in the room helping you craft your story! I can't recommend it highly enough! *Melissa Tagg, multi-published romance author*

# How to Write a Brilliant Romance

*How to*
**Write** *a*
**Brilliant**
**Romance**

Best-selling, award-winning novelist
and writing coach
Susan May Warren

**Why do fools fall in love?**
The easy, step-by-step method of crafting a powerful romance

The easy, step-by-step method of crafting a powerful romance

What does it take to write a brilliant romance? Susan May Warren knows exactly how--and you're about to find out.

Now, for the first time, she's revealing her step-by-step romance writing secrets that will show you how to craft an award-winning romance.

**Secrets like:**

- How do I structure my romance?

- How do I create likeable heroes and heroines?

- How should my hero and heroine meet?

- How do I make two characters fall in love?

- How do I write a sizzling kiss?

- How do I create believable conflict?

- How do I keep the tension high in the middle of my story?

- How do I put romance on every page?

- What is the breakup and why do I need it?

- Most importantly, how do I create an unique romance that touches the heart of my reader?

**Find the answers to all these questions as well as a few secrets to creating award-winning romances.**

With ten ingredients and step by step instructions you'll learn how to plot and write a powerful, layered romance designed to win readers. Susan May Warren has coached hundreds of writers into publication, onto best-seller lists, and onto the awards platforms. (And she lives what she teaches. Susan is the bestselling author of over 50 novels, has won the Rita, the Christy, and the Carol awards multiple times.)

Did you like this book? Thank you for reading!

I love to help authors with their craft, encouraging them and
equipping them with tools to get published and stay published. I do hope you enjoyed our "conversations" and that they
helped you as you grew your story.

If you're interested in more resources on writing craft, or even growing your career as a novelist, check out our website:
www.mybooktherapy.com. Sign up to receive the daily dose of writing craft, and check out our programs and/or events. We have something for everyone!

If this book clicked with you, I'd be ever so grateful if you'd
share that with me (susan@mybooktherapy.com) and others by way of a review on Amazon.com.

**Go – write something brilliant!**